The Telephone Marketing Book

Better Business Guides

Getting to YES
Roger Fisher and William Ury

Effective Delegation
Clive T. Goodworth

Janner's Complete Letterwriter
Greville Janner QC, MP

The Basic Arts of Financial Management
Third edition
Leon Simons

The Basic Arts of Marketing
Second edition
Ray L. Willsmer

The Telephone Marketing Book

Pauline Marks
Managing Director of Pauline Marks UK Ltd

Business Books
London Melbourne Sydney Auckland Johannesburg

Business Books Ltd

An imprint of Century Hutchinson Limited
62-65 Chandos Place, London WC2N 4NW

Hutchinson Publishing Group Australia (Pty) Ltd
16-22 Church Street, Hawthorn, Victoria 3122

Hutchinson Group (NZ) Ltd
32-34 View Road, PO Box 40-086, Glenfield, Auckland 10

Hutchinson Group (SA) (Pty) Ltd
PO Box 337, Bergvlei 2012, South Africa

First published 1986
Reprinted 1987 (twice), 1988

Set in 10½ pt Times by Mathematical Composition Setters Ltd
7 Ivy Street, Salisbury, Wiltshire

Printed and bound in Great Britain by
The Guernsey Press Co. Ltd., Guernsey, Channel Islands

British Library Cataloguing in Publication Data

Marks, Pauline
The telephone marketing book.
1. Telephone selling
I. Title
658.8'12   HF5438.3

ISBN 0-09-162910-1
ISBN 0-09-162911-X Pbk

Contents

Foreword 9

1 **Telephone marketing: the direct line to profits** 11
The changing marketplace – Cost of face-to-face calls –
Instant access – Cut costs on the path to increased results
by releasing resources – The facts – Why can a telephone
communicator make contact when a face-to-face
salesperson is unable to do so – The marriage of direct
mail and phoneselling – Flexibility of testing

2 **Making sure your telephone marketing department is
cost-effective** 22
We're here to make a profit – Response hours vary –
Improve or remove – Salespeople, not clerks – Call cards
– Computers – Payment

3 **How and when to choose and make good use of a
telephone marketing bureau** 28
Experience – Size – Marketing know-how – Guidelines –
Personnel – Procedures – The bottom line – When to
use a bureau – A gap in representation – Even with your
own in-house department it's worth considering a bureau

4 **Setting up an in-house telephone marketing
department** 33
Test first of all – Costs of the department per annum –
Setting up the department – How many chiefs and how
many indians? – Job functions – Recruitment – Records
– Analysing results

5 **Dealing with objections** 48
Probing and overcoming negative responses – When does
selling turn into harassment?

6 **Motivating through incentives** 53
Salary *v.* commission – Incentives – Salary plus bonus –
Contests – Individuals – General incentives –
Participation – Working conditions – Conclusion

7 **Lists: What is available to telephone marketers?** 58
Categories – Testing lists – Timing – Duplication –
Random dialling

8 **Scriptwriting** 67
Scriptwriters and word-pictures – Making the negatives
pay-off – Basic scriptwriting rules – 3-stages: telephone,
mail, telephone – Overcoming the secretarial hurdles –
What's in it for the prospect – Phrases that make
phoneselling easier – Closing a sale over the phone –
Overcoming resistance

9 **Incoming calls** 86
Freephone – RCF – DSN – Incoming call success stories
– Planning an incoming call service – Transcription

10 **Computerization and telephone marketing** 92
Integration of voice and data – Computer telephones –
Cost comparison – Call logging – Computer software for
Telemarketing

11 **The winning combination** 102
When the telephone call is the first stage – Phone-mail-
phone combinations – The personal approach – Test the
different methods

12 **Market research and the telephone** 114
Telephone sampling – Questionnaire construction for the
telephone – The use of the telephone, on its own or in
combination with other methods of data collection –
Final comments

13 **Seventeen ways to make the most of your phone** 121
1 As a substitute – 2 Testing a mailing list – 3
Fundraising – 4 Test marketing – 5 Investigation – 6
Testing campaign penetration – 7 Obtain qualified
appointments – 8 Repetitive selling – 9 Motivate lapsed
customers – 10 Preceding and/or following a direct mail

campaign – 11 New launch – 12 Sale of surplus stock – 13 Converting enquiries to sales – 14 Incoming calls – 15 Inviting the prospect to a seminar – 16 Political purposes – 17 Direct selling

Index 137

Foreword

It is a truism that the marketing world — or at least that in the UK — is divided into two distinct areas: those who understand telephone marketing and those who do not. And yet it is equally true that if ever there was a need for that world of telephone marketing to be openly appraised, assessed and analysed, now is that time.

For whilst direct marketing is now receiving the recognition many of its practitioners have been striving for so long to achieve (as evidenced by the establishment of separate direct marketing units by main-line advertising agencies; direct marketing Diploma Courses; expenditure of £450m per annum on what is now the third largest advertising medium) it is ironic that, until now, there has been only a limited amount of literature advocating the use and benefits of telephone marketing.

It is all the more ironic when one considers the growth of the telephone marketing industry. In the USA alone, over 2.5 billion telephone calls are made each year by direct marketeers, with Sears Roebuck, the huge mail order company, obtaining over $2 billion business via the telephone (almost ten times the volume received through the mail).

Today, in the USA, telephone marketing is growing faster than direct mail. And we are, I believe, about to witness a similar growth in the UK. For example, we now have the British Telecom Linkline system which, as its use increases to become a valuable consumer marketing aid, will result in more cost-effective telephone responses to press and television direct-response campaigns.

The direct marketing scene is therefore currently poised for a definitive work on this personal, professional — and often misunderstood — marketing tool. It is thus with dual feelings of pleasure and admiration that I have written the foreword to *The*

Telephone Marketing Book. Pleasure that, at long last, there is now such a straightforward publication devoted to this medium. And admiration for the way in which Pauline Marks has removed the mystique from telephone marketing so that its benefits, uses and versatility have become concisely defined and clearly described.

Here is a book for practitioners and users alike. It is not a book full of theories, but one full of practical, down-to-earth advice, proven ideas, suggestions and recommendations, and written in a clear, concise style – all the result of Pauline's unique experience in the telephone marketing industry.

This book is a veritable compendium of ideas for both beginner and seasoned practitioner alike. From the opening chapter on 'Telephone Marketing – the Direct Line to Profits' to the closing one in which Pauline Marks shares seventeen ways to make the most of *your* telephone, there is a wealth of valuable material for all. Read about the links between telephone marketing and direct mail; between the computer, incentives, and the script. And much more. You will find that Pauline's analysis is precise and prescient – and her recommendations practical and profitable.

It has given me a great deal of pleasure to write the foreword to *The Telephone Marketing Book*. A pleasure, I believe, you will share in reading it.

Graham R. Holland
London, November 1985

1

Telephone marketing: the direct line to profits

This book is addressed to everyone whose job it is to sell – and that means just about everyone in business anywhere. But business people, whether they have a product or a service to offer, aren't the only ones in the business of 'selling'; anyone who needs to communicate an idea to the public, or to convince it of the worthiness of some cause, is in the 'game of selling' too. That game, as we know, is increasingly, almost painfully, competitive today. What is more it is being played for higher stakes than ever before, and the costs of entering the field are rising every year.

There is, however, a way of reducing the cost of selling, releasing resources, and thus increasing profits sharply – a way which is relatively easy to master, infinitely flexible, and which produces results most marketing people find astonishing.

The marketing tool which leads to those increased profits is on everyone's desk, and is more familiar and accessible to us all than sophisticated computers and word processors in which business is today taking so great an interest. Yet that tool remains the most neglected, under-valued, under-used business device in the world. It is, of course, the telephone – and this despite the fact that to anyone with teenagers this generation seems to have been born with telephones in their hands.

Alexander Graham Bell would turn in his grave if he knew the way in which his invention is being ignored by tens of thousands of business people the world over. He would turn even more restlessly if he knew how *mis-used* his telephone has been by many who have tried to utilize it for business purposes without knowing how to do so.

Those marketing people on the other hand, who *have* made effective use of the phone have discovered economies and sales results which continue to amaze their company managements. They've discovered ways of using a proven, tried and tested marketing medium which cuts costs, boosts profits, develops new leads, reactivates lapsed accounts, and 'wins friends and influences people' with astonishing speed and efficiency.

There are many other tasks the telephone, if used rightly, can successfully undertake and we'll be discussing these in the pages of this book. All are cost-effective, and while they may surprise some of those who read these pages, they won't surprise the well-informed sophisticated business person who has had the good sense to dial his way to success in selling.

They don't surprise me either. I've been in the telephone marketing business for eight years, having pioneered phoneselling in the United Kingdom and elsewhere, alongside a 25-year career in direct mail advertising. I studied phoneselling in the USA, and, as you will see, successfully adapted techniques to meet the special needs of the British and European marketplaces.

Of course it was in the USA that Alexander Graham Bell invented the telephone and it was there that phoneselling was born. A few organizations tried to export it lock-stock-and-barrel to Britain, on the assumption that anything that worked in the USA ought to work in the UK as well. But, as many direct-response marketers had previously found, it was not possible to transport marketing techniques without making substantial adjustments for the different attitudes, needs and response mechanisms of the individual country. A certain amount of modification is always needed.

Common language does not equate with precise interpretations of thinking, acting, feeling and responding. Coca Cola may now be almost universal, but the ways in which 'Coke' is sold needs everywhere to be distinct.

So it came about that although the Americans were the forerunners of telephone marketing ways had to be found of *adapting* rather than *adopting* existing methods. It was soon apparent that although the American citizen received, and now expected, a certain amount of pressurized high-powered selling over the phone, his British counterpart, new to phoneselling, was completely adverse to receiving hard-sell solicitations. Having said this, it was also apparent, though, that the British were well-known marketers, not in any way adverse to receiving telephone calls providing that they were politely and justifiably structured.

Although the British were the second in the field of serious telephone marketers, the German and French swiftly saw the value in this new medium, and they were followed in quick succession by the Scandinavian countries, Benelux and the rest of the western world. I was given the opportunity personally of setting up telephone marketing divisions in Denmark, Australia, South Africa and Israel. In each country, the initial reaction was 'It will never work here − our people will resent the calls.' Yet in each country, telephone marketing is today working effectively and successfully in every sphere of commerce and industry.

The changing marketplace

The reasons for this universal success are evident if one considers the changing marketplace. For the ways in which companies promote their goods and services to the public are being dramatically affected by the changing world economy − even by world events.

Take just one simple fact. In January 1973 the price of a barrel of oil stood at $2.59 − about the price of a scotch and soda in a decent hotel or club today.

Then came the 'Yom Kippur' War in October 1973 and the Organization of Petroleum Exporting Countries (OPEC) doubled the price of that barrel to $5.17. Two months later, OPEC raised the price again, this time to a whopping $11.65 a barrel, an increase of almost 450 per cent in one year. Such oil price increases had the most devastating effect. Everything began to cost much more because manufacturing, processing and distribution industries all require energy − and the cost of energy in all forms was rising sharply as a consequence of the oil price increases.

Of course the marketing industry was profoundly affected. Media advertising costs, like other business costs, skyrocketed. For example, a full-page colour advertisement in *The Observer* now costs £8250 in contrast to £2950 in 1975 − an increase of 279 per cent!.

In September 1975, a month before OPEC raised the prices,

business postage bills also spiralled upwards, and by now seem to have soared out of sight. Within one short sharp decade between 1975 and 1985, postal charges in Britain rose by 129 per cent.

Cost of face to face calls

It wasn't, however, only in media advertising and direct mail that the marketing industry came to feel the effects of OPEC. The cost of maintaining a sales person on the road became so high that many profit-minded companies began to wonder whether there was any sense at all in keeping fleets of salesmen's cars full of petrol, and in meeting the rising expense of feeding and housing scores of representatives as they went their increasingly expensive way up and down the country.

A salesman on the road for a year now costs a company almost as much as does a small house. On average, a travelling representative is said to cost around £27,000 a year. If you multiply those figures to take into account the number of 'reps' in a sales force, the horrendous expense becomes painfully clear. If you then divide that expense by the number of customers even the most energetic sales person is capable of seeing in one day, then the cost per call becomes difficult to swallow and almost impossible to digest. Finally, if you divide the expense involved by the number of sales actually 'closed', then the cost per sale can often reach absurd proportions, especially if relatively low-price items are involved.

Sending sales people out on the road has, in many cases, simply become a luxury. Worse, it may actually be a hopelessly antiquated technique for many companies; one which ought now to be dispensed with as being lackadaisical and ineffective. Every further day sales people are kept on the road results in costs continuing to rise and a lessening of profits.

Instant access

Telephone selling can and does replace the old fashioned inefficient, horse-and-buggy approach. This new method ensures instant access to a customer, costs pennies rather than pounds, and lends itself to a flexible marketing strategy based on sound market research.

In short, the telephone is the most obvious sales tool of the modern age, an instrument we use throughout all our working days for every kind of purpose, and which we cannot afford to ignore when we devise our marketing strategies. All this is not new of course. Many successful companies have included telephone marketing as an integral part of their marketing mix for years. These include such household names as Walls Ice Cream, Birds Eye Foods, EMI records, IBM, Britvic, Time Life Books and Rank Xerox. There is no doubt that, subject to circumstances, telephone selling can do a better job, for less, than any other sales medium that exists.

Cut costs on the path to increased results by releasing resources

This headline is everybody's dream. It sounds too good to be true. Can one cut costs and increase results by releasing resources? The answer is *yes*. All the ingredients are there. Working on the axiom that the more contacts you make the more orders you receive, a telephone marketing promotion can swiftly completely cover an entire field of prospects for the product or service being offered.

As an example, let us look at the retail chemist trade. If you exclude multiples, there are approximately 10,000 independent retail chemist outlets. Necessarily they have to stock a very wide range of merchandise, and therefore they are probably subjected to more sales calls than most other retailers. Whilst the shopkeeper may very well welcome a salesman's visit during off-peak periods when perhaps he is bored and glad of an opportunity to chat, it is different when the representative is standing in front of his counter taking up valuable space to make his sales pitch – to the detriment of the paying customers who are waiting to be served. Often the irritation this situation causes a shopkeeper results in the representative being sent away empty-handed, when the merchandise is in fact needed to replace out of stock items.

Timing is very important. Based on the proviso that an average salesman can call on 10–12 outlets a day, it would need a salesforce of 24 in order to cover all the retail chemists outlets once every two months.

If, during the interim period, a salesman from a competing manufacturer visits the retailer, perhaps at the very moment his stock levels are low in the particular merchandise, it is quite likely that the rival company will receive the order from the retailer – who does not maintain high enough stock levels.

Had, however, that same retailer received a regular weekly telephone call, without doubt that same order would have been placed with the regular company. As a further rationalization of this point, consider the fact that a face-to-face salesman making his 10–12 calls daily would not expect to receive an order from each prospect he visited. An optimistic salesman would perhaps consider he could make 25 per cent sales. Therefore taking the average salary (plus) as £27,000 per annum, each sale will cost his company between £40 and 45. In this context it must immediately make good sense to use the telephone to obtain repeat orders where the product/merchandise is well known and the customer is fully aware of the range available. This does not mean that all a telephone communicator has to do is to call and ask if the prospect would like to repeat a previous order. The communicator should upsell to an equal, or greater, extent than the face-to-face salesman. After all, he has a great advantage. He is not standing in front of the counter or desk taking up valuable floor space; and most of all he has the undivided attention of the customer at the other end of the telephone.

Lead generation

Qualification by telephone marketing should be an integral part of marketing plans. The savings realized in making full use of an expensive salesman's time is substantial. If every call he makes is now to a definitely potential customer, then his order rate must increase and the overall sales (and profitability) improve. The cost of making the telephone call in this context is insignificant, particularly if the same call is used not only to provide a firm qualified lead, but also obtain other relevant information which can help.

By releasing the resource of trained salespeople, they can now be employed to do the job for which they are best qualified – opening up new accounts, and servicing major customers who justify such attention and will respond by placing more substantial business.

The facts

The telephone communicator works in a relaxed, friendly environment, unhampered by rain, snow, sleet, heatwaves, car troubles or the other problems with which the travelling company salesman is beset.

Four telephones, manned by trained communicators for 6 hours daily, for a 5-day working week, 50 weeks in the year, can effectively be expected to produce between 35,000 and 45,000 sales calls a year.

The telephone can stand alone, but when it is used in conjunction with other media of mass-communication, it will very sharply increase the effectiveness of each approach – either as a direct selling tool, or for market research needed to find the names and addresses of prospective buyers as well as their possible interest in the products and services being offered. I would stress here, as I do later in this book, that market research should never be used as a guide for selling – and the prospects on the other end of the telephone must always be told the purpose and reason for the call at the beginning of the approach, rather than at the end.

Used correctly, and ethically, information gained will quickly allow informed decisions to be taken on whether an expensive face-to-face sales person should call on the prospect. Moreover, it will frequently open the door for the salesman in those instances where he has previously been unable to gain entry.

Why can a telephone communicator make contact when a face to face salesperson is unable to do so?

Most of us are unskilled at 'getting rid of people' who we believe to be time-wasters. This is often particularly true of the small local retailer, insurance broker, estate agent or other service industry, whose reputation has been built on the friendly relations and good humour he extends to all comers. An unexpected salesperson who enters his premises is often, in a sense, an unknown quantity – the prospect simply cannot tell in advance how much time that person will take up, and subsequently he is loath to start a meeting with him. The telephone is different. If he is really not interested he will say so; if he is busy, he will not hesitate to agree to being called back at a specific time he designates; if he intends to place an order he can do so quickly and efficiently with the minimum of delay. He does not need to give a great deal of time to the transaction. This can be summed up by the following fact:

When the telephone rings, we all give it our immediate and full attention, no matter what; yet, when a sales representative calls upon us, we will interrupt his sales pitch to go and answer the phone.

There is no doubt which system gets top priority treatment everywhere, and at all times.

The marriage of direct mail and phoneselling

Sending glossy, printed sales literature through the post is costly – more so today than ever before. Sending it out 'cold' to an unknown list can at times be *very* wasteful, since it isn't until the responses come in that a company can gauge which of the recipients were likely to be interested in the first place. A mailing list of 1000 home-owners, for example, doesn't tell us much about their interest in buying swimming pools; it only shows that they own their homes and do so within a certain locality which is a prime area of swimming pool ownership.

Turning that same list over to experienced telephone communicators will produce more positive information. By skilled probing, they will reduce that list of 1000 home-owners to those who are truly interested, allowing the expensive mailing pieces to be sent only to those people who are likely to study the literature with the attention it needs, if the reader is to be converted into a buyer.

A pre-advertising telephone campaign will tell a company whether or not the name and address file it is holding is that of likely prospects; it also provides a valuable personal contact with the potential buyer establishing his needs and identifying particular areas of interest before the brochure and letter are put in the post.

Let us continue to examine the marketing needs of the swimming pool manufacturer as a case in point. His segmentation of the marketplace is necessarily small, and very difficult to pinpoint in a mailing list. Using pre-advertising techniques, an introductory call would include something on the lines of:

'As a homeowner, Mr X, I wonder whether you have a fairly large garden?' After all, if the man does not have a large garden, what would he be doing with a swimming pool?

Gerry Broidy, the very professional and experienced man once in charge of many of Time Life's telephone marketing divisions throughout the world, told me, that as part of Time Life's training to its communicators selling books, they had a large printed notice in the department saying:

If the man says he doesn't read, thank him for his time and cease the call.

This maxim is well worth remembering. If the basic needs are not there, it is essential that communicators cease the call courteously – and sooner, rather than later.

The swimming pool campaign would perhaps continue by commenting:

"If you don't already own a swimming pool, I am sure you would be interested in hearing more about the XYZ new heated swimming pool – and the very big value it would add to your house Mr X."

Mr X may immediately express an interest – or maybe he says 'no' right away. If he does say 'no', it is up to the communicator to probe the reason for the negative response – it could be money, no swimmers in the family, age or just a total lack of interest in owning a pool. The well-trained communicator will be able to evaluate the quality of the response she receives, and by careful continuation of the dialogue either note down the prospect as justifying further expense to interest him by sending out a mailing, or having his name and address removed from the prospect file for the product.

You will see from this that direct mail based on information received from an initial telephone marketing campaign, may be carefully targeted with the minimum of wastage.

After the literature has been sent (and received) a second follow up call may be made to obtain a firm qualified 'lead' for the salesman to visit the prospect.

Whether it is a swimming pool one has to sell, or a piece of capital equipment, the technique works consistently well. It can be used to renew subscriptions, re-open lapsed accounts – and sell just about anything. As an indication of the success you may expect, consider the fact that two telephone calls (pre and post mailing) enabled us to sell a £30,000 crane directly without even the need for a face-to-face salesman's visit!

Flexibility of testing

Media advertising campaigns are of course the brain-children of advertising agency creative people, but whether they work or not must often necessarily be left to chance. Once an advertisement is placed in a magazine reaching thousands of readers, the deed is done. Each reader is exposed to the same sales message, whether it motivates them or not, whether it is cost-effective or wasteful. The money has been allocated, and, all too often, the cash involved goes down the drain.

Not so with telephone selling. Flexibility is the key note here. You do not have to stay with failure when you use this medium. Scripts can be changed daily, or even hourly, approaches can be altered, and then altered again, as often as necessary until a cost-effective sales pitch is evolved and seen to be working.

No one is perfect; no one in the marketing business can justifiably claim to know exactly what arguments will sway most buyers, unless extensive market research is undertaken. For this to be tried with print advertising, or radio/TV commercials, is *extremely* costly. It means running ads with different approaches one after the other, until the accepted version is found. The production costs are obviously prohibitive.

In telephone selling, production costs are very little, and test marketing of various approaches can be measured in very few pounds.

Four different sales techniques can, for example, be tested on 100 prospects each, and the results can then be carefully compared. If approach 'A' proves three times as effective as approaches 'B', 'C' and 'D', then approach 'A' can be used with confidence right across the board and a profitable campaign can be launched. One might find that two approaches work equally well, but for different markets. You could obtain better results in the Home Counties with one test and the other could prove more effective in the North. In telephone selling, a company pays only for what it uses, but it must make quite sure that only the best possible approach is made through serious testing of all the possibilities.

We find that a test of *100 contacts* is adequate to validate the success of each script and that providing sufficient communicators are available, educated assessments are possible in just *one day*. No other medium can equal this test facility in terms of both speed and low cost.

2

Making sure your telephone marketing department is cost-effective

Don't run away with the idea that telephone marketing *must* be cost effective. This is often far from the case, and many large company managers who boast about the sales achieved by their telephone departments have not really evaluated the true costs. The best way to ensure that what you are achieving is a profit is to sit down and look at the two types of costs. The tangible and the intangible. These should be worked out on an hourly rate.

The tangible costs should include:

Overhead factor, square footage, lighting, heating, wear and
    tear of equipment
Telephone rentals
Telephone charges (calculated on meter units)
Communicator fees
Supervisory and management fees
List research
Printing; and
Clerical assistance.

Intangible could include:

Setting-up costs
Bonuses and incentives
Scriptwriting and re-writes
Involvement of management; and
Briefing.

Allowance must be made for the variable factors in telephone marketing; for example, the number of telephone meter units used will vary with time of day, area to which call is being made and length of time taken. The important equation to make is

$$\frac{\text{Cost per telephone hour}}{\text{Number of sales}} = \text{Profit}$$

In chapter 4, I have detailed recording systems and the logic for their use. These are logical not only in that they provide the information you require for costing but they also can easily be maintained and read by the manager and supervisors in terms of individual achievement.

Each communicator hour must be detailed in a controlled and careful way, and the records should be evaluated daily/weekly/ monthly in comparison with previous reports so that any deterioration in achievements is easily recognized. If everyone in the department dials three given calls one day, this can quickly become the accepted call pattern unless charts and records are not only maintained but evaluated regularly.

Targets should be based upon the achievements of the most successful communicator, always bearing in mind your hourly cost. The telephone manager must be made aware of the *minimum* sales required for profitability as well of course as the *target* figure. Where this is exceeded, there should be incentives given ceremoniously to the communicators, and less obviously but still tangibly to the supervisor involved.

We're here to make a profit

In our experience telephone sales managers often lose sight of the fact that they are in business for *profit* and that the records have to reflect this hour by hour rather than on a weekly or monthly basis. Weeks and months are too late for improvement in telephone selling and the manager's plans for the next day's approach to his or her staff must be based upon the results in front of him for the previous six or seven hours' work. It is the manager's responsibility to make any necessary alterations to see that the maximum profit is made per working hour by correcting inefficiencies or ineptitudes which are obvious from the records.

The first one or two days of any operation must be discounted. This is the intangible setting-up cost. It can take up to ten working communicator hours to find the right level of approach; the script must be adjusted as necessary – maybe alter the basic offer or produce alternative answers to objections which are being raised.

Response hours vary

In consumer promotions the records will indicate at which hours of the day the prospect is most likely to be at home to answer the telephone as well as the hours to avoid, namely, when it is very difficult to get permission for a full presentation to be made, although the telephone was answered. This depends upon the category of consumer approached; parents of young children are usually harrassed between 5 and 7.30pm and not responsive to any sort of sales presentations. Working couples are busy preparing and eating a meal and have the same attitude to callers at this time. Retired people, on the other hand, will often respond more satisfactorily at this hour than if they were to be interrupted during their favourite TV programmes.

Business call contact rates vary according to the job title of the person you are trying to reach and the type of company he/she represents. In our experience the higher echelon of management should not be approached either on Monday mornings or Friday afternoons. Middle management, on the other hand, are often more receptive at these times.

These are all facts that well-maintained records will indicate and allow the manager to alter his calling patterns so that any non-profitable hours are eliminated from the daily schedule and to increase sales by engaging more communicators to cover those hours in the day that prove most profitable.

Improve or remove

The achievements of the most successful communicators should be used as the next day's target, but in a well-controlled telephone sales department there should not be more than 15 per cent difference between the best and the least successful operator (excluding new staff) and the telephone manager must always remember the Golden Rule:

Don't carry dead weight. A consistent low level reduces the cost-effectiveness of the whole department.

It is so easy to think, 'I am sure he/she will improve. I'll wait another day before I ask him/her to leave.' That other day is one too many. Successful telephone communicators are competitive. They are encouraged to be so. If everybody around them is making constantly successful calls, they too are keen; when, however, a slow and inadequate colleague is near-by, their own pace and results slacken. No department manager should hesitate to remove the offenders: they knew what was required of them when attending the initial interview and this has been emphasized at training sessions.

Salespeople, not clerks

Clerical staff are essential in the telephone sales department. Your communicators have been trained and are being paid on the basis of their ability to sell – not to spend their time writing out lengthy names and addresses. Basic information should, whenever possible, be pre-prepared and the communicators taught to amend the records and write down the information whilst they are actually talking on the telephone. This function is helped by the use of earphones; however in many telephone marketing departments, such as my own, earphones are abhorred by the operators – both men and women – even though lightweight sets are now available from British Telecom. Laborious handwriting in between calls slows down operation considerably both by the time it takes to write and by increased fatigue and should be avoided. Although push button telephones are less wearing than the round dial type, it is a constant manual function which, by its very monotony as well as the movement itself, can be very wearing.

Call cards

When the same people are contacted on a regular basis, you can take advantage of the different automatic dialling systems available, such as the Post Office's *call card* system, where numbers are pre-punched and automatically dialled in consecutive order.

Computers

A micro is now so inexpensive that it is well worth providing communicators with screens, and having a programme prepared

Figure 1

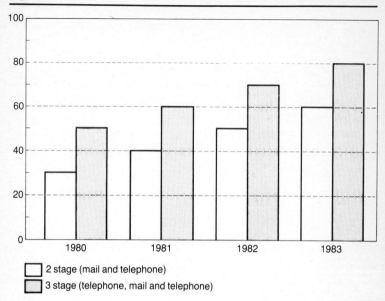

☐ 2 stage (mail and telephone)
▨ 3 stage (telephone, mail and telephone)

which will as far as possible allow for the operator to punch in maximum information using minimum codes.

To avoid errors, a single line of data at a time can appear on the screen, followed by validation. A competent programmer will ensure that the codes allowed maximize the possibility of detecting errors by building in check points.

Figure 2 Sample letter

Mrs Brown   Sabra Travel
211 Creighton Avenue,
Brighton, BN2 1RJ

Dear Mrs Brown,
Thank you for talking to me on the telephone today.

We are most appreciative of your interest in our exciting package tours, and immediately enclose a brochure so that you may lose no time in re-booking with us — and avoiding any possible surcharges.

SABRA Travel are quick to appreciate the value of your interest, and you can be assured of the same keen attention at all times.

Yours sincerely,
G. Gould (Director)

Using such a simple system, and combining it with a plotter, the end result could provide both pie-charts and histograms, and produce graphs which could for example show the resultant sales of a two-stage mail and telephone campaign, compared to a three-stage telephone, mail and telephone again (see Figure 1).

If a daisy wheel printer is used, it is also possible to dispatch a personally worded letter to each contact within minutes of the call being made (see Figure 2).

The communicator presses the appropriate key for an individual message and the whole operation is conducted speedily, highlighting the company's efficiency to the customer.

Payment

We have found that payment on an hourly rate is more conducive to consistent good selling in the initial stages of a communicator's employ than payment on a contact or sales commission scheme. Many good people who would have made excellent communicators are at first frightened at the thought of working on anything other than a flat rate, and others, not so naturally successful are possibly tempted to falsify their record sheets if they are getting paid only on results. In our 'Phonesell' department we find that a guaranteed fair standard wage initially gives confidence to the operator, who may then progress to bonuses and incentives, and occasionally be offered opportunities of working on a per-contact/sales success rate of pay scheme where they can prove their proficiency in the telephone selling skills that have been developed. Again, this must reflect in your hourly rate costs and be dependent upon your profit margin ratio to each sale made.

3

How and when to choose and make good use of a telephone marketing bureau

How do you go about it? Plunge in straight away, and base your choice on lowest price, or choose an agency because the sales manager is an amiable fellow who seems to know what he's talking about – or do you probe further?

First thing to do is to evaluate the sales manager's 'pitch'. If he is doing his job well – which is to sell to you – in the process he has to use every possible phrase in the book to make his operation sound attractive and successful.

Select a bureau in the same way you recruit new staff. Commence with a list of questions and by careful screening you narrow the field until you choose the candidate nearest to meeting your expectations.

If you already undertake some telephoning work in-house, you have a good idea of the questions to ask. In direct selling operations use your own operational field force as a measurement of the standard you expect to achieve.

As a further guideline, consider the following before making your final choice of bureau:

Experience

A new broom may sweep clean, but an older one has been broken-in and should certainly do a better job.

Check whether the bureau has experience in handling similar requirements to your own. Ask to see examples of the scripts used (in non-competing situations), and request a list of references. Don't be satisfied with one or two names. An agency in the business for more than two years should be able to provide a list of at least 20 clients for you to choose two or three names at random. Ask for details of the percentage of repeat business obtained and whether or not the bureau is involved in any repetitive or 'roll out' situations, i.e. where the client is so satisfied with the initial results, he asks the bureau to continue on a large scale.

Size of bureau

A key question is 'Are your telephones all in use everyday?' rather than 'How many telephones do you have?' A large installation does not necessarily mean a successful bureau – just that they have a great many telephones. Obviously, if the set-up comprises fewer than 25 telephones, think carefully before continuing. It could be that there are excellent reasons for such a small unit – or alternatively they could be unused to handling substantial volumes and will have problems in providing you with sufficient capacity. Telephone marketing is a numbers game, and a very competitive one. Four communicators working in a team will usually produce better results for you than two communicators working for twice the length of time. The very small bureau will probably cost less initially, but may well prove more expensive in the long run in relation to results achieved.

Marketing know-how

A good bureau will want to ask *you* a lot of questions too. Experience should provide them with the ability to hold an in-depth discussion on the place for the telephone in your particular marketing mix, and its economic viability for your specific purpose. They will need to know about your products, marketing methods and salesforce. A successful bureau will probably ask for a profile of your average customer, and should insist on a test of the scheme before allowing you to proceed with the whole campaign.

If the bureau is able to advise cogently on new list creation this is a plus when you are seeking to enlarge your customer base through cold calling.

Guidelines

The British Direct Marketing Association founded a telephone committee at my instigation in 1981. Bureau members of the

Council are not necessarily the best in the business, nor are non-members unworthy by default. All it means in effect is that members have agreed to subscribe to the guidelines laid down by the Association which ensure that calls are handled to a very high standard of courtesy and care. It is very well worth checking to see if the proposed company is a Council member – or alternatively if they do set themselves certain standards and practices. The BDMA Telephone Council is located at 1 New Oxford Street, London WC1 and they will gladly provide a list of members and a copy of the guidelines.

Personnel

Insist on meeting the key people who would be handling your promotion: The telephone sales manager, supervisor and, where possible, the team. Judge the company by their interest and enthusiasm towards your project.

Procedures

Look carefully into procedures. Will you be expected to brief supervisor and communicators yourself? If the answer is 'yes' this is another plus point.

Ask to see records currently kept, and check out reporting systems. If the system is computerized, make sure that there are adequate back-up facilities and any manual records are carefully maintained. Visit the offices. If the communicators are noisy without being loud, sell without harassing the prospects and the supervisor is on-the-spot listening to the calls, then it is very likely you have found a professional telephone marketing bureau who will assist in providing you with a profitable promotion.

The bottom line

How much should you pay and on what basis? There is no set pattern at the moment in the charges made by the different bureaux. Some charge by the hour. They will make the maximum number of calls for you during that period, and an initial test run should tell you exactly what to expect in terms of cost per sale, or per contact.

A setting up charge is usual. This will probably cover the briefing session, devising and printing and alterations to the script and any specific recording procedure necessary for your particular project.

Some bureaux charge per call, or by contact, or even by completed script. The first can be quite expensive as it may take several calls before an actual contact is made. Hourly rates often include British Telecom meter unit charges: other companies charge these out separately, either at cost or plus a small percentage.

All these factors need to be carefully checked, so that 'hidden charges' don't appear upon completion of the campaign – throwing the economics of the exercise into confusion.

When to use a bureau

One of the times it is essential to hire an outside bureau is when contemplating setting up your own division, as discussed in chapter 4. The wise, but inexperienced marketer will certainly test out procedures before committing him or herself to the expenditure involved in developing a new department.

A gap in representation

If you don't have a locum to fill a situation when the area representative has left, is on holiday or sick leave, the bureau can work quickly and efficiently to take orders and keep the area 'warm' until a salesman can make his usual visits. We have recently been involved in a situation where the sales manager of a very large specialist manufacturing company left his job to go over to the competition, taking with him many of the senior field representatives. Before they had a chance to get in their cars and approach previous customers for their new company, we had made 5000 calls appraising the same customers of the situation, offering goodies and firming up on brand loyalty. It was estimated that 95 per cent of the list remained with the original company. Our client, who operates an effective in-house telephone sales division, did not have the resources to make 5000 calls quickly – and his use of a bureau in these circumstances was justified.

Even with your own in-house department it's worth considering a bureau

Consumer calling is usually most effective after business hours and at weekends. It is often uneconomical to keep offices open at these times – and a bureau can be the answer in situations like this: as well as at times of overloading.

The criteria for employing a bureau must be 'when outside is either cheaper, better or more available than inside'. As a parallel, many companies with vast computer mainframe installations find it more efficient to use outside agencies in maintaining their direct mail files.

Fine tuning of your own department may well indicate that there are certain areas which could be cost-effectively sub-contracted to a bureau, releasing your own department for more involved projects requiring detailed knowledge of the product or service being sold. Functions such as reactivating lapsed accounts and updating mailing lists would probably be more efficient and cost-effective undertaken by an outside agency, whilst the in-house team is used to obtain orders and upsell to current customers.

Once you have established a good relationship with a bureau and they develop an awareness of your product or service, it is then possible to delegate specific work as the need arises with the minimum time loss or disruption of schedules.

4

Setting up an in-house telephone marketing department

We'll make do now and if it works we'll spend some money and set it up properly.

Whoa. Stop right there. It is *not* a question of taking a telephone, a clerk with some time to spare and a desk – and using this as a test operation. You need to know facts and figures which can only be obtained by running a full-time team dedicated totally to the project. So, apart from immediately expending £X thousand in setting-up an operation 'blind', how do you find out exactly what you can expect to achieve – in fact, the economics of the situation?

Test first of all

The answer is right-at-hand. Having decided on the functions of your proposed department, the prudent marketing manager will give a brief to two reputable outside bureaux and ask each to conduct a test campaign of at least 1000 calls on its behalf. If the objective is to use the telephone for more than one purpose, it would be wise to have a test conducted on each, as a separate issue. For example, you may wish to:

- Reactivate lapsed accounts
- Service low volume business
- Produce qualified sales heads
- Sell your product directly
- Find new prospects
- Undertake research

Brief the bureau exactly as you would your own sales people, and make it quite clear to each agency that you will want detailed information upon completion of the test.

Provide literature and point-of-sale material. Discuss your objectives fully and at length. Insist on meeting and talking with the communicators and supervisors who will be working on your project. Ask if you may visit the bureau whilst the campaign is taking place, and do so more than once if you can. A good agency will counsel you in depth, determining the position of telephone marketing in your media mix and working out with you an effective script and method of approach. Don't crowd the agency. Be content to let them formulate and test out various proposals so that you gain the full benefit of their experience. After all there is little point in paying for advice if you don't take it.

If you divide the test between two bureaux, it is essential that all the basic input provided to them is geographically the same.

Give each a section covering similar demographics, and time the operation so that it takes place concurrently.

When the tests are completed, the analysis supplied by each bureau should provide you with the answer to the question 'Will telephone marketing work for my company?'

Take the average of the information supplied unless there is a large discrepancy between the two figures in which case the test should be extended to a third outside source. As a general rule a difference of up to 20 per cent between the results of two agencies is quite acceptable.

Data needed from the test

1 Average number of diallings per hour per person
2 Average number of contacts made per person
3 Average number of meter units per contact − ask for two figures here − standard and peak rate calling
4 Actual number of diallings and total meter units overall
5 Positive responses
6 Number of those interested
7 Negatives
8 Detailed reasons for refusals
9 The 'nixies' (unobtainable or moved away) on your list
10 The most frequent objections received

Ask each of the bureaux for a 'roll-on' price per contact if they were to run the operation for you on a long-term basis. The information you received could look like this.

Report on telephone marketing test of 1000 contacts to client's list of lapsed customers

Duration of test	98 hours
Number of communicators	3
Total diallings	1440
Total contacts	989
Positive responses	137
Require further information	222
Negative	540
Need to be called back	46
Unobtainable	90
Total BTU meter units	7250

Reasons for negative responses (individually shown on scripts in detail

48% dissatisfied with service;

21% obtained better price from main competitor;

29% X Company rep visited more frequently and order placed with him

2% unwilling to comment.

Using the average figure obtained by combining the totals of the two bureaux, you will then be able to judge whether the cost of setting up an in-house division is likely to be justified by the results achieved.

Costs of the department per annum (£)

3 telephone rentals	500
BTU	13,000
Communicators salary (x 3)	26,000
Supervisor	9,000
Printing, clerk and computer time	10,500
Overheads and canteen	6,000
Setting-up and briefing	3,000
Scriptwriting and re-writes	4,000
Accounting, executive input	8,000
	80,000

With three communicators expected to make, say, 80 successful sales calls per week, the average cost to the company would be:

80 successful contacts × 3 communicators × 50 weeks p.a. = 12,000 successful calls
Cost per positive call = £6.66

However, most of the overhead costs would remain static for a larger number of communicators and the cost per sales call would be reduced accordingly. Compare your own costs to the 'roll on' figure quoted by the more successful bureau. If both are equal, and the cost per successful contact is profitable within your own financial structuring, you are on the right track and ready to begin setting up your department.

Setting up the department

Remember though that it is difficult to make a cake without breaking eggs. Referring back to the beginning of this chapter, don't fall into the trap of trying to 'make do' by using existing staff with time to spare. Consider these *don'ts*.

Don't employ people your personnel department are trying to 'offload'.

Don't employ the MD's niece who wants something to do.

Don't even think about the not-so-good salesman who wants 'a change' from being on the road.

Start at the very beginning. Where is the department going to be located? A bright room with natural light is essential. Invest in a thick pile carpet, and ensure that the walls and ceiling are soundproofed as much as possible.

Cork is an ideal top material for the walls. As well as providing additional soundproofing, it will allow for point-of-sale materials, notices and other information to be easily affixed.

Good ventilation and heating are particularly important in a telephone sales department, as well as easy access to a canteen for drinks and smoking. In our firm we allow a 20-minute 'break' in every 3-hour session. This can be taken in one, or offered as 2 breaks of 10 minutes each. Somewhere to hang outdoor clothes and lockers must be provided, and communicators should be discouraged from bringing newspapers and any other bric-à-brac into the room.

Rules are necessary and should be simple but firmly maintained. For example, in our firm we stipulate:

1 Hours of working
2 Canteen break details
3 No smoking
4 Outdoor clothing to be put in lockers and no items other than handbags allowed in the room
5 Drinks and food to be consumed in canteen only
6 Punctuality essential
7 Method and time of payment
8 The in-house telephone number to be given out to those prospects wishing to call back
9 Conditions of employment

An easel and board is an important piece of equipment and forms the focus of the room. Information on each particular project, individual results, and incentives should all be displayed on the board.

The names of the communicators should be written up daily with their successful results immediately marked up either by the supervisor as they are achieved or by the communicators themselves. Either way this provides excellent motivation for the communicators. We all like to be seen to do as well, if not better than, our neighbour, and will strive harder if our results are not as good.

Don't install desks. These encourage unnecessary clutter and mess. Plain 6' × 4' tables are sufficient, with triple filing baskets on each one to hold the paperwork. Depending on the number of people in the room, the tables need not be separated. Where there are eight or more communicators, the ideal grouping is in lots of four. This encourages motivation through propinquity: and a good supervisor will make sure that there is a more successful communicator acting as pace setter in each group.

Chairs should be comfortable, with good back support and without arms. We find that cloth coverings are better than vinyl which can get sticky in warmer weather.

Plenty of shelves are needed for telephone and other directories and the books should be meticulously maintained in alphabetical order. It is possible to place a permanent order with British Telecom for new issues of the telephone books as they are published.

As the bulletin board is the focal point of the room, all of the communicators should be faced accordingly; and a desk should be placed at the side of the board for the supervisor.

How many chiefs and how many Indians?

A department of four people does not justify more than one manager to supervise, maintain records and produce the daily analysis. Employ more than this number of communicators and you will need to have both a manager and a supervisor on the team. If the sole function of the department is to contact existing customers and your list is readily available together with telephone numbers, the manager will be responsible for making sure that there are sufficient contact forms available for each day's calling. Where the intention is to open up new prospect files, it may very well be that you will need to employ a clerk to research new names and addresses and verify telephone numbers. The latter is a laborious and time-consuming job which should not be given to the communicators − whose function is to talk to as many of your prospects as possible within a working day.

Job functions

The Manager

WANTED

Sales Manager, Public Relations Officer,
Personnel Manager, Administrator,
Analyst

The successful telephone sales manager needs to be able to combine all of these jobs. He must be capable of administrating a department competently, hire and fire fairly, motivate enthusiastically, produce analysis accurately and provide management with projections promptly and with foresight.

There aren't many trained people around already skilled in these attributes who have previous experience as a telephone sales manager. The industry is too new. If you are unable to head hunt, I suggest you look at two other possibilities.

1 Consider interviewing assistant sales managers, or very experienced field representatives, who have successfully worked and been trained by thorough organizations such as IBM. An enthusiasm to get into telephone marketing management, coupled with a good sales background, can result in first-rate administrators. Check carefully into previous involvement with records and give a plus point where the applicant has some knowledge of computer techniques.

2 You will almost certainly receive applications from telephone communicators who think they would make good managers. Don't dismiss them lightly. Contact the previous employer to check on success rates, punctuality, accuracy in filling out records and ability to get on well with other members of the team.

Supervisor

Although it is easier to fill the position of supervisor than it is to hire a manager, the supervisor should have the ability to maintain existing procedures, yet be flexible enough to alter requirements as needs arise. An important element of the job is to communicate with the operators so that the specific objective of each campaign is clearly understood.

The supervisor should be capable of running the training and re-training programmes and be completely au fait with the scripts, objections and answers, as well as having an accurate understanding of the number of diallings which could reasonably be expected to be made by each communicator.

'Warning bells' should ring in the mind of a good supervisor as soon as there is a lessening in the number of diallings made or results are not as good as previously. Steps should be quickly taken to re-motivate, improve scripts or re-train.

The supervisor should have first-hand knowledge of having worked as a telephone communicator, and because of this it is often possible to promote from an existing team.

Communicators

What kind of staff should I employ? Full or part-time? There are two schools of thought there. Personally I find that part-time personnel make better communicators. Working a 3-hour shift only, with a 20-minute break, under a competent supervisor, it is easier to sustain the necessary three E's which make a vital and satisfactory department:

Enthusiasm

Energy

Effectiveness

Part-time people may be housewives, students, actors ('resting' members of the acting profession make first-rate communicators) or anybody else wishing to work three hours a day, such as one-parent families. An interesting part-time job is not easy to obtain, and we find that staff employed on this basis are more anxious to work and keep their job than many full-time employees, although there is considerably more movement in 'coming and going' and length of employment tends to be for shorter periods than full-time staff. On the other hand, full-time staff have a greater tendency to develop company loyalty and are generally more committed to the job.

In chapter 2 I had the drastic sub-heading 'Improve or remove'. This really upset a telephone marketing consultant asked to give an opinion on this book. He implied that my attitude was too tough in this respect. Believe me, anybody who runs a successful department will tell you that it pays to 'fire' poor communicators sooner rather than later. Unless there is an obvious improvement in the approach and achievements of a particular operator, it is essential to dismiss the offender quickly for the well being of the whole unit. Good telephone communicators are competitive people who will try and improve on the results achieved by their neighbour. One person consistently producing lower results can easily de-motivate and lower the average throughout the department. The 'wait and see' manager who is hesitant to terminate through kindness (or lethargy) often lives to regret his action.

Be fair though. Make the position quite clear at commencement of employment. Explain the average diallings currently achieved, and the expected results. Speak plainly about the company's policy of hiring and firing, and the reasons why it is not possible to stay with failure. We monitor each communicator for two days after training is completed; if after this period of time the results are not within 50 per cent of minimum expectations, we immediately dispense with the operator's services.

Recruitment

If you decide to employ full-time communicators the usual avenues of newspaper advertisements etc. are the best place to do so. For part-time staff try *The Stage*, local employment offices and university personnel officers. We have had many excellent communicators who have worked on a part-time basis for three or four years whilst they have been at college.

The first and main interview should be by telephone. The form illustrated in Figure 3 has been deliberately designed to encourage the impatient candidate who has insufficient patience to be a communicator to show visibly his irritation at the inanities and format of the questions asked. If the candidate comes over well at this first interview, there should be a 90 per cent possibility that you have a good communicator in the making. Forget about everything else, when you finally come face-to-face for the second interview. One of the best communicators we ever had was an elderly lady who wore white gloves and a picture hat throughout the day, yet consistently turned-in high verified sales results. Another young man wore different coloured wellington boots everyday and his waist length hair was tucked into a cummerband. He was our most successful communicator for a whole year. Had these interviews been face-to-face rather than by phone, there is no way at all that either of these people would have been employed in the bureau.

Sometimes, particularly when showing visitors around the department, I feel that we are operating with ex-employees of

Figure 3 Interview form

PAULINE MARKS TELEPHONE INTERVIEW FORM

INTERVIEW TIME IF SET AFTER THIS TELEPHONE INTERVIEW	Date:
	Time:

"I'm sure you have some questions about the job, but first let me ask you some questions about yourself."

How did you hear about the job?

1. Name _____ Phone _____ Today's Date _____

2. Address _____ How long at this address? −( ) +( ) over six months / less than six months

"We're at _____ How far is that from you? Travelling time from us? −( ) +( ) less than 20 minutes / more than 20 minutes

3. Last job _____ How long were you employed? −( ) +( ) more than 1 year / less than 1 year

Pay at last job? −( ) +( ) more than £7,500 p.a. (£150 per week) / less

How many employers in last 5 years? −( ) +( ) less than 3 / more than 3

Can you write clearly? −( ) +( ) yes / no

4. Job Skills

Have you ever sold anything?

$-(\ )$ $+(\ )$ yes

no

INTERVIEWER
Rate quality of phone voice.

$-(\ )$ $+(\ )$ very good

less than very good

5. Total $-(\ )$ from above _____. If more than 3, say "Thank you for your interest in the job, but we have had others apply that have had more of the experience we are looking for."

If less than 3, say "I have just a couple more questions I'd like to ask before we set up an interview for you."

6. Are you looking for part time work? $(\ )$ Yes $(\ )$ No

7. The starting pay is _____ per hour. Would that be acceptable to you? $(\ )$ Yes $(\ )$ No

8. The job mainly involves communicating with business people over the telephone at their place of business. We have an excellent training programme. Does this sound like something you might be interested in? $(\ )$ Yes $(\ )$ No

9. If the answer to Nos. 6, 7 & 8 is yes, say, "It sounds like we should discuss the job further. Could you come in at _____ for a personal interview with _____?

He will answer any questions you might have at that time.

the Barnum and Bailey Circus – yet if we shut our eyes and listen to the enthusiastic and melodious voices, I wonder instead whether we may be employing ex-members of the Royal Shakespeare Company.

Records

Once you have employed the communicators, and immediately embarked on a carefully planned and controlled training programme, it is essential that you have clear recording procedures before the operation actually starts.

Records are particularly important in a telephone marketing department. They immediately indicate weak spots, and read carefully, will foretell impending problems. They take the guesswork (and possible bias) out of management, and are totally essential to the success of the whole campaign. Without an effective recording system it is difficult to maintain growth and make the best possible use of available resources.

The best record system must be one which is simple for the communicators to maintain, and easy for management to analyse and use to improve performance. The information

Figure 4 Communicator's daily call report

Communicator				Ref			
				Date			
Hours	Diallings	Contacts	Positives	F/1	N/1	N/R	N/E
1	25	10	3	4	2	1	—
2	26	9	3	2	1	2	1
3	20	8	1	2	1	4	—
4	26	11	4	—	3	4	—
5	25	10	3	2	—	5	—
6	22	8	1	1	1	5	—
TOTAL	144	56	15	11	8	21	1

Note
F/1 – Further Information required
N/I – Not Interested
N/R – No Reply
N/E – Non existent

obtained should increase profitability by clearly pinpointing areas in which results are falling behind the general trend and enable management to rectify the trouble. It is only through good recording that it is possible not only to improve a situation, but, even more importantly, to obtain a clear understanding of what the problem actually is.

There are always 'high flyers' in every telephone marketing department, and the differential between their results and 'Mr Average' can be as high as a 2:1 ratio. In a well managed office the 'high flyer' is carefully used as a pacesetter whilst at the same time every effort is made to see that the extraordinary results are used to motivate rather than to discourage the average operator.

Most successful departments run on an hourly basis and the communicator's call record card could look like the one shown in Figure 4.

Analysing results

Presuming that the operator is working from 10am to 5pm with a one-hour lunch break between 1pm and 2pm, it becomes obvious to management that the third and last hours of the day need re-vitalizing. Fewer diallings have been made with the result that there are fewer positive responses. The answer here is to motivate by incentives during these periods. Usually we offer a cash payment for the most positive responses, together with a different incentive for the largest number of diallings made. This gives an opportunity for both the high flyer and Mr Average to exceed their previous totals and re-motivates the whole department.

The other message immediately apparent from the record card in Figure 4 is that more prospects are unavailable in the afternoon for this particular project. The answer here ideally is to eliminate the afternoon session and double up the staff for the morning period when more prospects would appear to be available. This is not always practical in an in-house situation, and the solution could be to extend working hours to test response from an evening or weekend session.

It can happen quite legitimately that a communicator will work for a three-hour session and not achieve any positive results. It can happen, but it is very rare and should not go unchecked. It is not unknown for an operator to falsify the number of diallings made, but use of call-log or similar computer equipment will verify each report as well as provide the number of BTU. If the reason is not through tardiness in making too few diallings, the trouble must lay with the method of presenting. In any event, accurate and frequent reading of the records will enable management to rectify the problems.

One card cannot be taken in isolation. Totalling all the records on an hourly basis will produce average figures for each period, and at the same time indicate those communicators producing less effective returns. BTU (meter units) should also be evaluated against each individual's results. This could show that some communicators are holding lengthy conversations without results – or the reverse could also be true.

The individual records should be entered onto a master sheet, which again should be as simple as circumstances allow (see Figure 5).

It may be that you are using the telephone marketing department to obtain leads for salesmen or for research such as product, price, seasonal or demographic testing. Perhaps you intend to sell directly. All of these functions need separate call reporting; and the emphasis should always be to produce the least complicated sheet necessary, coupled with an effective filing system. Salesmen's leads need particular attention and the

Figure 5 Weekly management call record card

Date _____ Comments _____

	Diallings	Contacts	Pos	F/1	N/1	N/R	N/E	Total hours worked	BTU
1									
2									
3									
4									
5									
6									
Total									

Figure 6 Weekly management sales leads report

Date _____ Comments _____

Total leads issued this week:

Cumulative total of leads:

Advised as contacted:

Outstanding to be contacted:

Salesman	Leads this week	Cumulative	Contacted	To contact
A				
B				
C				
D				
E				
F				
G				
H				

weekly management report (see Figure 6) should show the exact position encompassing both the figures produced by the communicators and the follow-up by the salesforce.

I always recall with horror the 150 timed and verified appointments within one month made throughout the Greater London area for one company. The job was undertaken through their agency who 'forgot' to let us know that the client's salesforce was reduced to just two. The result was that 100 expensively acquired 'leads' were totally ignored. With a weekly information report in front of management, danger signals can quickly be read, not only by the sales manager, but also by the telephone manager who can either increase the operation as necessary, or reduce the number of leads being obtained pro tem until the field force catches up.

If the telephone manager and the sales manager are one and the same, there is not any difficulty in obtaining this information – but in a larger organization problems of communication do occur (and in not-so-large companies too). It's worth inviting everyone's cooperation at the outset. Point out the truth of the matter. *Everyone*, including the individual sales person, benefits from clear accurate records.

5

Dealing with objections

'What is in it for me?'
'What's the catch?'
'I really don't need it...'
'Can't afford it at the moment...'
'I'll think about it'
'I have to ask the boss/wife/colleague'
'I've managed without one so far'
'Call me next week'

There are people who object to Margaret Thatcher, to the colour of your carpet, the car you're driving, the holiday tour company you are going to travel with, and probably even the colour of your socks. Maybe they'd even object to the colour of your underpants if they knew it. So, don't be surprised if they object to your telephone solicitation. It is after all totally in character.

You don't have to be a 'professional objector' of course to say 'no' automatically to a telephone (or indeed any other) sales presentation. The communicator's skill comes in defining the true reason for the objection.

There are really four possible objections to any sales situation.

'I can't afford it' (Lack of money)
'I'm in no hurry' (I'll buy later)
'I have no need' (What will I do with it)
'Not interested' (Lack of confidence)

A good sales presentation is designed to draw a few 'yes's' from the prospect. This is done to make it easier for him or her to say 'yes' at the time it counts most. Never consider the possibilities of asking someone if they are interested. This is always sudden death! You put the prospect on the spot with this approach by giving him a choice of *yes* or *no*, something or nothing. Always ensure presenters offer a choice of *something* and *something*. Put the pressure on the product rather than the prospect. Instead of 'Would you like to buy Tower Bridge, Mr Brown?' the correct approach is 'Would you prefer Tower Bridge or Windsor Castle Mr Brown?'

Bearing in mind that the prospect will not particularly wish to be sold, he will certainly appreciate an opportunity of making a choice. Beware, though, never to give too many choices; this can be self-defeating.

If a customer tells you he won't see the rep this time round, he is waivering. The *benefits* should be used as an inducement, possibly emphasizing the limited availability or keenness of the price structure — and endeavouring to get across the message that any delay could be giving up a golden opportunity. The main negative reasons or objections should be known immediately, as a result of an initial test of the telephone campaign, combined with knowledge obtained from the company's records and salesforce. These should form part of the original briefing to the communicators, and they should always be provided with a list to which they can refer.

The simplest method is to mount some small plastic envelopes measuring around 16 × 11 cm onto a cardboard approx 27 cm square. The end result will be an easily accessible flip-up chart (see Figure 7), which will assist the communicators to *sell the*

Figure 7 Objections

If prospect objects to the proposal, probe the true reason and refer to the appropriate response.

Can't afford

I'll think about it

Don't really need it

I have to ask the wife/husband

Thinking about it

Call back next week

Competition is better

benefits of the programme and reinforce their memory in emphasizing the key points of the promotion.

The objections voiced by the prospect are not always the true reasons for saying 'no'. People do not always say what they mean – or indeed mean what they say.

The communicator must probe as skilfully as possible, seeking clues to the true reasons for the negative reaction to the proposal, by encouraging the prospect to talk and discuss the offer in greater detail. The right questions carefully structured beforehand, and continued (but not extensive) dialogue will usually indicate the exact reasons for the refusal.

'Don't really need it' could mean that the benefits have not been clearly understood, and the communicator should re-emphasize the value of these. Alternatively the prospect may really be saying that it is too expensive for his current budget. The answer to this problem should be conveyed as an additional benefit, particularly if there is a form of easy-payment scheme available.

'Thinking about it' or 'Call back next week' could just be a polite way of saying that the prospect was not interested. The communicator should instead treat this type of response as an opportunity of reinforcing the sales pitch by answering with 'Yes, but ...' and repeating the benefits.

Probing and overcoming negative responses

It is more than likely that the reason for the initial lack of enthusiasm is because of the communicator not convincing the prospect that they should take the decision to buy *now*.

If there is an exceptional benefit to offer, the telephone marketer should not be afraid of repetition, and interject these as answers to any interruption during the presentation.

An important and essential way of overcoming objections is by having confidence in the product or service being sold. It is a rewarding experience to listen to someone who radiates with confidence. He or she sounds sincere, attentive and interesting. The person *believes* in his product, *believes* in his company and *believes* in himself. The prospect will rely on his judgement. Trust him, want to buy from him. Communicators must have a positive and enthusiastic attitude in order to convince those who are reluctant to buy. Above all they must not fear explaining the costs involved in purchasing the product they are trying to sell — but rather *emphasize its worth* to the prospective customers.

'I have to ask my boss/husband/wife' should be pursued by the communicator with 'Yes, but *you* do agree that the XYZ typewriter is just what you need, don't you Miss Brown?'

If Miss Brown agrees, the next stage is to try and get her consent to make a reservation subject to approval of the third party.

With your permission, I will reserve an XYZ typewriter for seven days at the special rate for you. If your boss doesn't agree that an XYZ will not only make work more pleasant for you but also produce professional letters to a very high standard, we will of course cancel the reservation immediately. If this is agreeable, I will call back in seven days and you can let me know his decision.

The same objection could also mean that Miss Brown was not the correct decision-maker to contact, and tactful questioning should lead to the name of the person responsible for purchasing new equipment.

'I've managed without one so far' Yes, but ... his competitors haven't and they are doubtless highly delighted with the additional business it brings them.

Mrs Brown may still be taking her washing to the launderette, and explains that at £1 a week, she can use the service for five years for the cost of the washing machine the telephone marketer is trying to sell to her. Yes, Mrs Brown, but ...

The inconvenience when the weather is bad, or wasting summer evenings and weekends sitting in the hot, stuffy launderette

Of course a machine in your own home means that the only washing which goes into it is your own and your family's

So much whiter, more hygienic and readily available

Once it is paid for, the cost is nil. We operate an excellent service maintenance contract, and the average life of *one* machine is *12* years.

A washing machine in your own home is almost a status symbol. There are X per cent households with them in your TV area.

Talking the points through and encouraging dialogue will 'prod' the prospect into revealing the true objections and give the communicator every opportunity to reply with the predetermined responses.

When does selling turn into harassment?

If the lady is 87, she won't want to buy life insurance! The border line between hard-selling and trying hard to sell is a very narrow one, and communicators must be taught the importance of not stepping into the dangerous area of 'pushing' a sale too much. Not only may such action actively damage the seller's image, it can also result in a disproportionately high level of refusal to accept goods, and subsequent denials of agreements made on the telephone.

Benjamin Franklin said 'Lose no time. Be always employed in something useful. Cut off all unnecessary actions.' Once a sale is made congratulations are in order. This is a success story, but being a good loser is part of the selling game, and if a negative response is still received after all benefits have been repeatedly stated, and there is no indication that the prospect may change his mind, it makes good sense to close the call quickly and courteously and to start again as soon as possible with the next person on the list. Time wasted is money down the drain. Always remember that telephone marketing is a numbers game – the more calls made, the higher the number of orders received. There are no success rules that will work unless this is always borne in mind.

6

Motivating through incentives

Good morning communicators. These are your calls for today. I expect at least 20 diallings every hour. Good luck. Get to it!

And there you are. In front of you is a script and a pile of telephone numbers. You face the prospect of spending the next few hours dialling, repeating the same message, concluding your 'spiel' and then starting all over again.

Frankly the job is tedious. You don't see the face of the person to whom you are talking, and unless some interest in the form of an incentive is introduced, the boredom you feel is reflected in your voice to the detriment of the success of the telephone calls being made.

In order to overcome this problem it is necessary to implement means of motivation by developing strategies which will interest the communicators and encourage them to treat each prospect as an individual call rather than as just one of the day's production.

Salary *v.* commission

It is very advantageous to the manager in those situations where a firm-cost-per-hour is negotiated to pay a definite salary to the communicators. It also enables the supervisor to ensure a certain level of output and most importantly it negates the aggressive 'hard' sell which can actively damage a campaign if the situation is allowed to get out of hand. An effective communicator being paid per order or for each appointment achieved will usually produce better results than if paid at an hourly rate. When analysing the final results, however, it is often found that orders acquired by aggressive telephone selling are frequently cancelled and appointments made in this way often do not end in sales – possibly because the prospect feels that they have been forced into a situation against their own judgement. The communicator may also be tempted to create leads with unqualified prospects.

Conversely, whilst personnel are generally happier to have the assurance of a guaranteed level of income, it also means that, generally speaking, they will not make the effort to reach higher levels of productivity. This lack of effort or malaise can lead in turn to mediocrity and a lowering of standards.

Incentives

There are a few people who are motivated by pride in achieving good results. For most, however, this is not enough. The ideal method is to produce a structure that provides for a regular hourly payment, but also incorporates a performance award. This need not necessarily be money, although ideally it should be a combination of both.

We discovered that in the sixth hour of making commercial sales calls (between 4 and 5pm) we were achieving a lower rate of diallings – and, subsequently, the number of contacts and sales – than during the rest of the day. Enthusiasm had obviously flagged by the last period.

For five days, half the team were offered an incentive for the sixth hour. Comparative results for the same project showed:

	Without incentive		With incentive
	Hours 1–5	Hour 6	Hour 6
	Average	Average	Average
Diallings	364	298	370
Contacts	152	90	152
Sales	10	7	11

By using an incentive scheme, 24 per cent extra diallings resulted in a 69 per cent increase in contacts made and a not surprisingly 57 per cent improvement in sales, Indeed, often as in this instance, the sixth can become the most productive hour of the working day.

The incentive need not necessarily be money. It can be a bottle of wine (a great favourite), an umbrella, sunglasses or a large box of chocolates, maybe even a theatre ticket – or something else of this kind of value. Often, in order to re-kindle flagging enthusiasm, the supervisor makes a 'mystery' out of the incentive by writing the description on a piece of paper, folding it over and then pinning it to the board.

Salary plus bonus

Providing that the hourly payment is a reasonable one, the telephone manager can realistically hope to achieve and maintain a certain level of production by offering bonus payments for all contacts made above a minimum level.

If costings are worked out on the basis of paying the communicator say £4 per hour for an expected ten contacts, then by making a bonus payment of 40p for each contact in excess of this number the net effect is an incentive to increase production whilst maintaining cost per sale/enquiry.

This system needs detailed bookkeeping: but as long as the bonus does not exceed the hourly payment, it does not lead to 'hard' or aggressive selling.

Contests

There are many variations to the ways in which you can motivate a telephone marketing sales department. Pitting teams against each other brings out the competitive side of most people. Lunch for the winning team is a very acceptable reward, and pizzas and beer brought into the offices always bring 'crowing' noises from the winning team and encourage the unsuccessful communicators to 'beat' their colleagues the next day.

Individuals

Individual incentives can effectively be offered for

Best results in a particular hour
Most contacts in a working day; and
Highest diallings in a period (needless to say more diallings lead to a greater amount of contacts and subsequently increased sales).

Lots of small incentives are more effective than large prizes. The latter, in any event, would nearly always be won by the same people each time. Every telephone marketing department has its 'high flyers'!

Lots of incentive prizes means that all the communicators will or should win something and this creates an excellent incentive for everybody to excel.

As an example, whilst selling a milk drink to 10,000 potential retailer outlets, we found that sales in the third and fourth day increased by 40 per cent. The satisfying result was due entirely to a very bright telephone supervisor who instituted a form of pass-the-parcel. This consisted of passing round a sealed envelope from communicator to communicator. They could only keep the envelope whilst they were actually talking to a prospect. The manager had pre-set an alarm clock, and, when the bell rang, whoever was holding the envelope was able to open it. Contents varied between £1, £5 and £10.

Number of diallings increased dramatically. Nobody wanted to miss out on a chance of holding the envelope. Perhaps the telephone supervisor was too good. He was subsequently headhunted by our client!

General incentives

Whilst it is wise materially to motivate in terms of immediate gain, there are also other ways of rewarding enthusiastic personnel. In-house promotion creates an upward mobility within a company which encourages the more ambitious communicators to strive for a higher level of production in order that they can be offered the same opportunities.

Obviously there can only be few vacancies for supervisory and management jobs. However, a department can be run on two or more levels with payments adjusted accordingly. Providing that the schedule can be worked out accordingly, the first level could be straightforward list research, customer service repeat calls, etc. and the second section would be more complex with the communicators being rewarded accordingly. Promotion from one area to the next is excellent motivation and creates a competitive atmosphere which eliminates the lethargy which can otherwise creep in with drastic results.

Participation

Successful scripts should always have been tested first of all before the roll out commences. The best way to test a script is to invite the participation of the communicators to criticize and suggest improvements based on their personal knowledge of the response achieved during the initial calls. This will create a team of involved people, who feel that they are an integral part of the company, contributing towards its success. This is the very best motivation of all.

Working conditions

Good incentive schemes need to be backed up with clean and relaxed working conditions: pleasant decorations, comfortable chairs, telephones which require minimum effort to use 'easy dials' and lightweight receivers. Adequate lighting is important, and ventilation. A stuffy or cold office is not conducive to encourage enthusiasm amongst personnel.

A break of 20 minutes is essential in each three-hour period, as is a place to have a drink and smoke a cigarette away from the telephone room. This also gives the opportunity for communicators to establish a comradeship which encourages them to stay with the company and to feel part of a team rather than just individual employees.

Conclusion

Telephone marketing is all about communication. People talking to people on the telephone every day. It is not a production line, and a good department should reflect this in the enthusiasm and concern of its personnel. Motivation by use of incentives is an integral part of the structure which is justified by substantially higher production through enthusiastic participation by the communicators.

7

Lists: What is available to telephone marketers?

The very best list you will ever have is the one that is already in your files – your existing customers. The next most successful should be your file of lapsed customers, with the enquirees who have not yet proceeded to order third in line.

Telephone marketing to all three of these categories will not only keep them 'live' but can reactivate the second and remotivate the third category in a very cost-effective way. We all like to go where we are welcome. The *maître d'hôtel* of good restaurants have the right idea. They flatter us by remembering our names and personally welcoming us to their establishments. When we leave they thank us for our custom. The result is that we will go back time and again to that same restaurant. Exactly the same reaction can be achieved by telephone marketing. Flatter your customers and prospects by contacting them by name and asking for their custom and there is every likelihood that you will achieve your objective.

Of course your existing file of names and addresses is not sufficient to obtain new business. It is necessary to obtain an exact profile of your average customer – just as if you were conducting a direct mail campaign – and use this as a base for acquiring further lists.

Categories

If your needs are in the industrial and commercial fields, you will probably be able to obtain the categories you require from a published source. There are many good directories available, including *KOMPASS*, published by Kompass Publishers Ltd, East Grinstead, West Sussex and an excellent list of around 2700 commercial and industrial publications carefully indexed by CBD Research Ltd, 154 High Street, Beckenham, Kent.

Whilst not all the registers and books give telephone

numbers, quite a large percentage do so – and of course it is much easier to find the telephone number of a business than of a consumer.

I say published source, rather than a list broker because, with few exceptions, industrial files are generally computerized without telephone numbers being added. List brokers too are very diffident about supplying names and addresses for telephone marketing, and although this position will necessarily change over the next few years, the situation is presenting a problem at the moment to many telephone marketers. However, the following are a selection of lists being offered in this way, subject of course to the individual company's conditions of contract and availability. Their inclusion in this book in no way recommends the lists as particularly suitable or successful for any particular project.

IBIS Information Services Ltd
Waterside
Lowbell Lane
London Colney, Herts
0727 25209

This organization offers a computerized business file consisting of 130,000 named individuals in over 90,000 UK companies. They quote 80 per cent of the list available with telephone numbers.

Quantity breakdowns by standard industrial codes, area and size of company is given in Table 1.

Mailist Ltd
62 Lower Redland Road
Redland, Bristol BS6 6SS
0727 737763

The following are some of the lists available:

Description	Quantity
Companies who sponsor sport	450
Computer owners	6 500
Wealthy at home address	86 000
Dairy farmers	1 300
Cattle breeders	450

QUANTITY BREAKDOWNS BY AREA, SIC AND SIZE OF COMPANY

*Regions	Number of Employees	A000	1000	2000	3000	4000	5000	6000	7000	8000	9000	Total
Greater London	Over 400	7	48	113	234	218	61	144	106	280	57	1268
	200-400	6	23	56	165	189	40	100	75	135	22	811
	50-200	20	66	173	652	736	98	337	244	417	212	2955
	0-50	20	81	153	567	830	76	639	431	2700	606	6103
South East	Over 400	9	44	160	451	220	104	146	89	179	85	1487
	200-400	8	25	129	383	279	82	141	54	118	50	1269
	50-200	23	64	420	1528	888	223	595	301	321	502	4865
	0-50	51	81	388	1661	1354	234	1521	817	4540	1049	11696
South West	Over 400	5	22	48	113	104	30	33	23	41	28	447
	200-400	3	10	46	124	100	37	49	11	42	12	434
	50-200	9	18	132	453	366	99	295	131	116	93	1712
	0-50	17	26	111	415	484	64	1314	307	1661	545	4944
Wales	Over 400	—	14	32	45	21	13	11	8	16	25	185
	200-400	1	8	16	62	36	8	16	5	12	11	175
	50-200	7	15	81	185	134	32	73	51	50	57	685
	0-50	8	23	77	214	233	40	722	161	791	227	2496
West Midlands	Over 400	6	20	114	346	110	40	61	16	100	25	838
	200-400	3	6	99	278	106	33	54	20	39	7	645
	50-200	12	24	344	1277	479	94	288	113	159	114	2904
	0-50	9	29	225	1132	547	86	611	281	1581	344	4845
East Anglia	Over 400	2	8	17	46	58	17	12	11	19	19	209
	200-400	1	9	9	42	41	18	21	13	12	11	177
	50-200	6	8	46	200	156	29	73	72	37	41	668
	0-50	12	5	55	222	213	32	291	156	604	218	1808
East Midlands	Over 400	6	20	54	127	162	31	44	17	41	19	521
	200-400	1	15	31	108	164	22	39	12	32	9	433
	50-200	12	23	119	410	585	76	161	94	90	81	1651
	0-50	5	32	94	330	586	54	390	219	910	251	2871
Yorks & Humber	Over 400	11	31	130	239	228	55	77	49	82	27	929
	200-400	5	16	66	143	205	47	79	28	40	16	645
	50-200	8	29	262	670	683	146	384	131	105	93	2511
	0-50	13	51	299	682	957	227	1065	375	1428	326	5423
North West	Over 400	4	14	98	198	194	32	73	34	92	32	771
	200-400	4	11	75	146	255	33	69	30	49	23	695
	50-200	9	39	271	694	821	93	306	169	174	119	2695
	0-50	12	45	333	831	1092	100	880	505	2015	410	6223
North	Over 400	2	10	59	100	70	38	19	31	43	19	391
	200-400	4	3	27	54	55	29	18	20	17	8	235
	50-200	12	25	107	194	136	59	123	77	69	52	854
	0-50	8	16	80	192	242	47	510	190	737	205	2227
Scotland	Over 400	4	31	38	86	121	58	50	41	43	29	501
	200-400	8	8	70	96	114	30	52	23	17	15	433
	50-200	26	35	167	410	475	105	305	153	69	120	1865
	0-50	21	28	135	361	529	81	2125	286	761	524	4851
TOTALS	Over 400	56	262	863	1985	1506	479	670	425	936	365	
	200-400	44	134	624	1601	1544	379	638	291	513	184	Grand
	50-200	144	346	2122	6673	5459	1054	2940	1536	1607	1484	Total
	0-50	176	417	1950	6609	7067	1041	10068	3728	17728	4705	
		420	1159	5559	16866	15576	2953	14316	5980	20784	6738	90351

SIC GROUPS (header spanning A000–Total)

* For definition of regions please see map over page.

AREA

THE BUSINESS FILE IS
SELECTABLE BY
- **COUNTY**
- **METROPOLITAN AREAS**
  WHICH ARE SELECTABLE
  SEPARATELY FROM THEIR
  OWN COUNTIES (AS
  INDICATED BELOW)
- **LONDON IS SELECTABLE**
  BY POSTCODE

Bulb growers	35
Fruit growers	1 120
Turkey farmers	140
Garden contractors	510
Charities, mostly named secretaries	1 200
Associations, mostly named secretaries	3 250

Pauline Marks Direct Marketing Ltd
Pembroke House   Campsbourne Road
London N8 7PT
01 348 4294

The following are some of the lists available, all with named executives:

Mail order textile buyers	30 000
Accountants practices, named partners	11 000
Architects, individuals	20 500
Civil engineers	44 000
Bank head offices	250
Building Society head office and branches	250
Estate agents	9 000
Doctors	74 000
Transport and travel – full breakdown	24 000
Antique dealers	5 500
Brokers	10 180
Solicitors' practices	10 500
Directors, by company, geographically	115 000
Middle management, by type of job and company	200 000
Telex owners	76 000
Dentists	22 100
Opticians	5 840
Public utilities, by type	2 200
Surveyors' practices	8 400
Retailers, by trade – geographically	350 000
Manufacturing, by trade and number of employees	45 000
Wholesalers, by trade – geographically	36 000
Professional list – total selection	18 000

CCN Systems Ltd
Talbot House
Talbot Street
Nottingham N91 5HF
0602 410888

This firm is currently adding telephone numbers to their 40 million consumer file which is based on the electoral roll. This can be matched against ACORN, and could prove invaluable to telephone marketers.

Testing lists

When considering using a list, you must always bear in mind that telephone marketing is a numbers game. The more calls you make, the more prospects and subsequent sales you will achieve: and a substantial allowance has to be made for sufficient numbers to be available for engaged signals, gone aways and heavy call-back situations.

Out of every 30 diallings, we expect to make between 7 and 10 contacts for industrial promotions, and between 10 and 15 for consumer campaigns (dependent of course upon the accuracy of the information in the file being used).

One of the many advantages of using the telephone to market your product is that you can easily and quickly test not only the script, but also the actual list before you commence to roll out.

To quote an example. A mail order company purchased a large quantity of good quality suitcases. These were considered too up-market and expensive for their usual C1/C2 mailing list, and they decided to try and sell by a combination of telephone and mail to a completely 'cold' file. The first list they rented was a file of people who had booked a holiday cruise. The profile appeared to be the correct one, and it was decided that some 12,000 persons would be contacted, in a two-stage promotion. Firstly by mailing-out an attractive folder; secondly a telephone marketing call endeavouring to obtain an order. We persuaded the company to test the list beforehand and prior to the mailing, the telephone was used on a small sampling of 500 random names from the file. Two facts emerged immediately. The incidence of 'nixies' on the list was disproportionately high at over 10 per cent and the prospects were unanimously not interested in the product. The main reason for this was that the list was made up primarily of first time cruisers who had taken the trip within the previous two years, and on that occasion had bought new suitcases to embark with on their holiday.

As an alternative, the mail order company rented a list of people who were known to fly regularly. A similar 500 random test proved that the file was acceptably accurate with 2 per cent 'nixies' and the positive reaction to the proposal justified a roll-out situation, which in fact achieved a very satisfactory level of 6.3 per cent orders, against a break-even requirement of 2.5 per cent.

Whilst it can be a mistake to be too selective, it is a much bigger mistake to rent large lists without first testing. There should not be any delay in testing by telephone, and very little cost. The availability of being able to 'put a toe into the water before jumping in' must be regarded as a bonus for every marketing director.

Geography can be an important factor. Suburban listings may produce better results than urban simply because shopping by post may be easier when there are longer distances to travel – and the local retail outlets may not have sufficient variety of merchandise. In other instances the reverse may be true.

Think carefully about the quantity of names you may need. There is little point in renting a list of 100,000 if you have only four communicators. By the time they reach the end of the file, it will necessarily be out-of-date.

The direct mail industry has always been conscious of the problem of unwanted mail and in March 1983 a mail preference scheme was set up. Members of the public are invited to write in using Freepost 22, and receive in return a full explanation of the service. 27,438 people responded in 20 months. Of these, 22,841 followed up by requesting that their names and addresses be deleted, and a surprising 2356 actually asked for their names to be added-on to the files of all subscribing members.

With their thoughts turning in the same direction, the BDMA's Telephone Council is currently discussing the formation of a similar scheme.

Individuals who make known their objections to any form of telephone solicitation will have the opportunity of asking to have their names and numbers removed from the files of companies subscribing to the scheme. Obviously, there will also be the opportunity to request an 'add-on' to all available files.

Timing

Failure of a campaign to succeed may not be because of the list. The timing of your telephone calls must be carefully studied and based not only on an evaluation of the original test, but also on knowledge of outside influences. There is, for example, very little point in telephoning a GP during the morning when he is in his surgery, or, contacting a company director at 6 o'clock on a Friday evening when he is anxious to get home for the weekend. Conversely, there is every reason to believe that you are likely to reach a high incidence of farmers at 5.30 pm on a winter's evening, or be able to contact schoolteachers at their homes during school holidays.

A great deal of thought should be given to the lifestyle of the prospect. You may well be self-defeating in promulgating a programme of telephone marketing to parents of infants, if your telephone marketers make contact between 6 and 7.30 pm when the housewife is particularly busy putting the children to bed. At the same time you can irritate the man of the house if you telephone during the Cup Final, or some other shattering world event! It is not always possible to be aware of these circumstances, particularly in cases where the campaign is directed universally rather than to one location, but the keen supervisor should pick up on the situation quickly and will wisely call a halt to the promotion.

Duplication

Avoid duplication like the plague. Nothing annoys a prospect more than to be called twice, unless it is (horror of horrors) to be called more than twice. If your list comes off the computer, your own or anybody else's, make sure that it has been run through the de-duplication programme, not only for the exact name and address, but also taking out more than one different name at the *same* address and telephone number. Nowadays it it is not unusual for two people to live together, unmarried but as one household, and two telephone calls are almost never justified in those circumstances. The situation must be particularly looked at when a list is split between various communicators, who would not have any means of realizing that the prospect had already been contacted.

Random dialling

Random or sequential dialling is used a great deal in the USA, and to a degree by certain direct sales companies here. It is hazardous and not to be recommended either ethically or in terms of achieving a successful campaign.

Subscribers who go to the trouble of ensuring their numbers are not listed in the telephone directories do not regard telephone solicitations favourably – and such calls would kindle a reaction which is in all the industry's interests to avoid.

On the subject of random dialling, by machine, Sir Gordon Borrie, Director General of Fair Trading in the OFT Report on Telephone Selling published in October 1984 commented:

British Telecom has confirmed that it remains opposed to the use of random or sequential call diallers on the grounds that this would place an intolerable burden on the existing cable network.

The Office therefore remains strongly opposed to the introduction of automatic dialling equipment in the UK unless there are adequate facilities to enable people to avoid receiving such calls should they so wish.

The BDMA's Telephone Committee unanimously agreed with the importance of this comment, and the guidelines contain a firm commitment to the sentiments expressed on this subject by the Office of Fair Trading.

8

Scriptwriting

Script? Oh no, not for us, we don't want our communicators to speak parrot fashion!

Quite right. You don't. Let's make it quite clear from the outset that a script is to be used as a *guideline* – not as a straitjacket. It is meant to be a help, and ought never to be a sacrosanct document to be kept to at all costs, word-for-word.

We've all watched admiringly as the best of our stage and TV actors and actresses manage to ad-lib 'perfectly', i.e. to suit the mood of the audience and the needs of that special moment. The most skilful always seem to radiate warmth and sympathy. Well, that's the way it ought to be with a telephone communicator too. The script is necessary to make sure the most salient points have been covered and the meaning of the message remains the same – but it needs to allow flexibility. It has to give your best communicators freedom to 'ad-lib'.

That freedom also extends to particular phrases within the script.

Because all people are – thank heavens! – different, some of them will find difficulty in saying particular phrases. Forcing them to utter these puts them right into that 'straitjacket' against which we warned earlier.

Take, as an example, that American way of ending a conversation with, 'Have a nice day!' It so happens that I personally find it particularly pleasant, but I do know that our own communicators feel embarrassed by it. Asking them to use it would be just ridiculous. They don't feel right about that phrase, and, because of this, they would distort the words and meaning.

The point of 'Have a nice day!' is, after all, to end a conversation pleasantly, and that can be done with a phrase which British communicators find more 'natural'. So long as the conversation ends pleasantly, it doesn't matter, after all, how the call is terminated – whether it's with 'Have a nice day', or 'Well, I'll say goodbye and thanks', or even simply by, 'Thank you for your time.'

The point is, once again, to make sure your script allows for flexibility. Demanding anything else is not only silly, but unrealistic too. Even if you did insist your communicators stuck to the script, they would deviate from it after the first hour or so, finding phrases they felt were more 'natural' to them.

Scripwriters and word-pictures

The playwright Luigi Pirandello once wrote, 'Six Characters In Search of an Author'. In just the same way, your communicators – and the message they're meant to communicate – are in urgent need of an 'author' – a scriptwriter. So where do you find one? And who is likely to be a good scriptwriter?

Let's begin by weeding out those who won't fit the bill. They include a lot of people who might be regarded as logical candidates for the job. But, without special training, the following won't qualify:

- your direct mail copywriter;
- your advertising agency's copywriter;
- your company's star marketing and/or sales director; and
- that clever fellow or girl who usually writes your company's sales pitches.

The fact is that a scriptwriter has to be trained in the fine art of producing word-pictures. A moment's thought will show you that this is a very special writing – and selling – skill.

Any form of writing other than scriptwriting can be accompanied by an illustration or picture of the product. Much the same is true for other forms of selling. Your salesman can produce samples, take a prospect to a demonstration, or at the very least show a leaflet. Moreover, the salesman has the added benefit of using facial expressions, gestures, even bodily attitudes ('body language') to illustrate and emphasize the points being made.

The telephone communicator has only words.

Let's see what those words have to do −. the kind of job they're meant to perform.

In order to illustrate this, let us suppose for a moment that you, the reader, are office manager of a company employing, say, 75 staff, and that a salesman has called in at your firm's reception, asking to see you about 'Bloggs Photocopiers'.

You're not really very interested, but you agree to see the sales representative anyway, perhaps because you have a slack moment, or maybe because you feel you ought to keep abreast of what new photocopying equipment is available on the market.

The sales rep immediately makes a good impression. He has a nice appearance, a pleasant, honest face and you are quite impressed when, after firmly shaking your hand, he asks for permission to demonstrate the machine he has left in his car − entirely without obligation, of course. In due course he has set up the machine on a corner of a desk in your office, and you can see that it looks good and works well.

Understandably, however, you can't make up your mind then and there whether to buy it or not, and so you ask the rep to call again after you and others in your company have given the matter some further consideration.

That sales call has probably cost Bloggs Photocopiers Limited around £45.

A telephone call could have achieved the same level of interest in the product and ensured a definite appointment for a demonstration at a *fraction* of the cost. Moreover, an appointment arranged by telephone would certainly have put the onus on the prospect to proceed with the purchase.

In order to accomplish this, however, your telephone communicators would have needed to use a script which provided an attractive word picture − one which would have had to be painted something like this:

The Bloggs Photocopier is an ultra-modern machine, beautifully designed and finished smoothly in aluminium painted silver grey... It's so compact that, at just 18 inches-by-18 inches, it can sit at the end of anybody's desk... and it's so easy to use that even the errand boy can run it without any problems at all.

Making the negatives pay off

Selling by telephone demands a re-think of your sales techniques and even of your product. Why, for example, do your salesmen get turned down — when they do? What arguments do they encounter most frequently? What are the chief objections they hear, time and time again?

Take a full briefing from your company's sales people. They are, after all, the ones most deeply involved in your product or services. They're the troops on the firing-line, the ones who receive all the 'flak'. It's the job of management to know what that 'flak' consists of.

Your salespeople can provide you with a list of the reasons prospects give for not placing an order. These reasons are ammunition for you. They're the 'objections' you need to incorporate into your script, along with the answers most likely to convert them into a sale. If a company has a large sales force, so much the better; management should talk to as many sales representatives as possible, and then collate all the information they provide.

At the end of the exercise, you should end up with a paper which looks like this:

Objection	Positive Response
'We've already got a photocopier.'	Yes, but the Bloggs machine is so inexpensive it will pay you to have another one in your office.
'The budget for this quarter has been spent.'	In that case I suggest we reserve a machine at today's price and deliver to you, say, May 1st?
I'll never have another Bloggs! Our last Bloggs machine kept breaking down.'	Yes, but that was before we developed the model 73X. Over 1500 machines have been installed without complaint. Quite a record don't you agree?
'We'll think it over and let you know.'	May I suggest that you reconsider and place your

order now, as there is a once-only discount of 15 per cent which is only available till the end of this month.

And so on and so forth. Whilst the objections are not strictly *part of* the script, they have to be readily and immediately available on a separate document or flip-chart, so that the telephone communicator can refer to them easily.

Basic scriptwriting rules

1 *Talk to the right person*
The opening gambit should always be directed at making certain that the voice at the other end of the telephone belongs to *the* key person – the decision-maker.

2 *Be open and above board*
Telephone communicators should introduce themselves by name, detail the company they represent, and briefly indicate the purpose of the call being made.

3 *Let the prospect comment*
The script should allow for plenty of pauses, giving the recipient of the call an opportunity to make comments and allowing the telephone communicator a chance to estimate the initial reaction.

Remember: pauses are *not* hesitations!

4 *Soft-sell*
In order to establish a rapport with the prospect and to ensure his or her cooperation in allowing the conversation to continue, *always* obtain permission beforehand. A very effective way of doing this is to use the opening phrase, 'May I just have 60 seconds of your time to tell you about....?' Our experience proves that very few people refuse to listen for just one minute, and that is enough time for a communicator to project a 150-word story about a product or service.

5 *Word pictures*

This is the point where your 'word-pictures' come in – coupled with the 'benefits' to the prospect. It is quite helpful when initially writing scripts to dictate these benefits and those word pictures onto a tape, then to play the tape back whilst you shut your eyes and imagine yourself at the receiving end of such a conversation. The benefit *to the prospect* must be told at the beginning of the script.

6 *Give your communicator the chance to listen*

Your script should provide for pauses to allow your telephone communicator to gauge reactions, and then either continue with the call plan if the response has been positive or allow the communicator to refer to his or her 'objections' sheet, if a negative answer has been received.

7 *Make it positive*

The script should always allow for definite affirmative responses. Instead of saying, 'Would you like a representative to call upon you next week, Mr Brown?', the script should be re-phrased to put the question this way: 'Which day of the week would suit you best, Mr Brown – Monday, Tuesday, Wednesday, Thursday or Friday? Or are weekends more convenient for you?'

In the same way, whenever you are direct selling, always assume the larger quantity. In other words, rather than saying, 'How many would you like?', say, 'I am sure you will want to take advantage of the 20 per cent discount we offer on 12 gross packs, Mr Brown.'

Finally, leave little opportunity for the recipient of your call to say 'no'. Always give positive alternatives: 'Is it 12 gross or 24 gross, Mr Brown?' and 'Would Thursday or Friday be a better evening for the kitchen furniture salesmen to call, Mrs Smith?'

8 *Keep to the point*

The commitment to a time, quantity, or request for a brochure is really the *close* of a script. Do not overextend this! The lengthier you make a script, the more chance you stand of losing the attention of the listener, and the less time the telephone communicator has to make the next call.

Don't get too involved in trying to explain all the whys and wherefores of the product or service you offer, or attempt to detail very involved pricing structures, where for example you are offering various models. The aim of the script on these occasions should only be to gain the interest of the prospect and his or her agreement to receive a detailed catalogue or make a firm appointment for your sales person to visit.

Leave plenty of room for comments. All good telephone selling should have a strong element of a research questionnaire in it. If the answer is 'no', make sure you find out *why*.

Write the script in the same way as you would talk to a new acquaintance to whom you were hoping to sell. Eliminate any phrases which make your pitch sound phoney. Cut down on the effervescence. Comments such as 'I am absolutely delighted to speak to you' impress no one and are usually immediately rejected by the prospect.

9 *Ask the right questions*

When planning your script, make sure that your initial questions give a good opportunity to your trained telephone communicator to probe, so that he or she will quickly learn from the responses received whether there is a qualified prospect at the other end of the phone.

10 *Have at least two objectives*

A call need not necessarily be 'wasted' if the primary objective is not immediately achieved. Leave room within the script for lesser objectives.

For example, if the prospect is not interested in placing an order for the six shirts you hope to sell him, leave the way open to send him a catalogue and get permission for a further call to be made after he has had a chance to look through it.

11 *Testing*

One of the bonuses in telephone marketing is that it provides a company with the ability to test and test and test again. The telephone is the one medium in which you do not have to stay with failure – unlike radio and television commercials or print media, where once you have placed your advertising message, you have to live with it.

Testing extensively by telephone is *not* costly. After a good writer has completed his first draft of a script, he can select 100 names at random from a proposed list of targets, and then get his best telephone communicator to make contact with these, using his initial script. Analysing the reaction will determine what if any alterations are needed in the script, and this is a process which should continue until a satisfactory set of responses is received.

The section that follows looks at some typical scripts and telephone marketing situations. In each case, the scripts cover a different area, but all are actual. They have all been used successfully and each has been developed after careful initial testing.

Do you think, for example, that the product or service you offer is too technical to be sold by phone? This might indeed be the case – but *only* if you are trying to 'cold sell' a highly technical product. If, on the other hand, you use the two or three-stage approach described in chapter 11, 'The winning combination', then it is *not* impossible. Take the case of a company promoting the sale of air compressors – not an easy product to promote, as you'll agree. Yet a *very* successful three-stage telephone/direct mail/telephone campaign was conducted, using the following script (into which we have incorporated instructions to the telephone communicator using it):

3-stages: telephone, mail, telephone

Stage 1: Initial telephone call

Good morning/afternoon, may I please speak to the person within your company who would specify the purchase of air compressors?

At contact: Good morning/afternoon, Mr Brown, my name is Tom Jones, calling on behalf of the XYZ Company about our range of special air compressors and ancillary equipment. We will be sending your company some information about this and would like to confirm that you are the correct person with whom to liaise.
(If not, find out who the correct person is and repeat. If not applicable, indicate reasons why.)

Stage 2: Personalized direct-mail is then sent to the named specifiers

Stage 3: Second telephone call

Good morning Mr Brown, this is Tom Jones of the XYZ Company, I recently fulfilled a promise to send you some information about our special air compressors.
(Pause for comment.)

Our technical representatives would like to call and discuss the benefits of the product in greater detail. Can I arrange that he calls upon you Monday of next week, or would you prefer Tuesday/Wednesday/Thursday/Friday, am or pm?
(If negative, probe.)

Is it for budgetary reasons you do not wish to see a technical representative, Mr Brown, XYZ operate a very economical leasing scheme, which coupled with the advanced technology of our new equipment, is guaranteed to save you money.
(Refer to list of objections and responses.)

Overcoming the secretarial hurdle

The vast majority of secretaries and PAs zealously guard their bosses. After all, this is part of their job, and the following techniques are useful in order to penetrate the screen they throw around their employers.

If you're following a mailing campaign

Refer to the correspondence; 'I'm calling Mr Brown to discuss the letter I recently sent him.'

Assertively

If the secretary insists on finding out your reasons for wanting to talk to her boss, be assertive: 'I feel sure Mr Brown would wish me to talk directly to him.'

By-pass the barrier

Many executives start work earlier than their employees. If you try an early morning or late afternoon call, you may well get through directly.

Use long distance as a reason

If you are calling outside your town, mention this fact as a reason for being connected quickly. 'This is Paul Jones calling long distance for Mr Brown. Can you put me through right away, please?'

Overcome unavailability

If the person you want is at a meeting, or otherwise engaged, get an indication of a time when he or she will be available and make sure you call back then. 'I am phoning Mr Brown at this time, as we arranged....'

When endeavouring to reach business executives it is essential to develop these persistent formulas in order to obtain maximum exposure to the key decision-makers.

Telephone sales techniques of course vary, according to the needs of the programme.

An example is provided by a holiday group which wished to sell their programmes directly into working men's clubs and associations. As these 4000 clubs are spread sparsely up and down the country, the cost of sending a sales force was obviously uneconomical, particularly as club and association secretaries, or organizers, are usually available only during very limited periods throughout the year.

The holiday group turned to telephone marketing and a very successful phonesell exercise resulted, despite the fact that it was necessary to make as many as three or four call-backs to contact the correct person.

Figure 8 shows the script we provided for our telephone communicators in this exercise. Out of a total of 4000 clubs and associations, we contacted 3500 club secretaries and organizers. Of these, 81 per cent agreed to receive information. We have been advised by our client, 'XYZ Company', that conversions to solid bookings exceeded 10 per cent.

Total cost: £12,250

Total bookings for current year of exercise: £320,000 – with the added benefit of a roll-on situation for subsequent annual bookings.

Look again at question 6a, where the communicator is asked to probe the reason why the prospect doesn't want literature. The reason could be anything. Maybe he just doesn't understand the offer being made to him. That, too, happens. A few probing questions and a presentation of benefits can alter an attitude and promote a desire to learn more about the product or service the telephone communicator is offering.

Figure 8 Sample script

---

1 You will be speaking to working men's clubs/associations. Ask for *the person responsible for organizing trips and holidays for members:*

Contact name, including initials ⎯⎯⎯⎯⎯⎯⎯⎯⎯⎯⎯⎯

Title ⎯⎯⎯⎯⎯⎯⎯⎯⎯⎯⎯⎯⎯⎯⎯⎯⎯⎯⎯⎯⎯⎯

2 'Good afternoon/evening. My name is ⎯⎯ and I am calling on behalf of the XYZ Holiday Group. I understand, Mr (contact name), that you are responsible for organizing trips and holidays for your members. Is that correct?' (yes/no)

3 'Have you ever used XYZ before?' (yes/no)

4 (If 'yes') 'Oh good! Then you must be aware . . . .'
(If 'no') 'That's a shame! Well, then perhaps you are not aware . . . .'

5 '. . . (aware/not aware) that XYZ is able to offer you holiday and leisure facilities which can be tailor-made to suit your requirements — either just for an individual member or for a group — and for the length of time you require.'

6 'I would like to send some information for you to look at showing our exciting programmes.' (Pause for comment).
a (If negative) Probe reason and offer benefits.
b (If positive) 'As we have so much to offer, and just to make sure that the literature I will be sending you deals with your specific needs, I should like to take just 30 seconds of your time with some brief questions:
  o How many members do you have?
  o How many usually join the holiday scheme?
  o Where have you travelled to these last three years?
  o What sort of holiday is most popular?
  o What time of year is preferred?
  o How much per head would you expect to pay?'

7 Thank him for his time and promise to send the literature in the post promptly

---

Probe: 'Exactly why aren't you interested in our holiday package?'

Objection: 'I've heard uncomplimentary things about your company.'

Reply: 'Our company? I find that incredible!'

The communicator has now established the reason why the prospect refuses out of hand to see the material being offered. If a probing question had not been asked the call would have been wasted and a sale lost indefinitely.

Any objection must *always* be answered immediately, even if it is only by means of a paraphrase of the prospect's own words.

Objection: 'You're too expensive.'
Reply: 'We're too expensive'.

Objection: 'There's no choice in your catalogue.'
Reply: 'You're saying there's no choice in *our* catalogue?'

Following the immediate response, the communicator must launch into the benefits, all of which should be separately listed and easily identified.

Objection	*Benefit*
'Your holidays are too expensive.'	'Compared with any of our rivals, we offer better prices £ for £ for quality accommodation.'
'We don't want to travel up to Heathrow Airport.'	'Of course not. our packages can be arranged from your local airport. That's Manchester, isn't it?'

Every telephone marketing campaign should be prepared on the basis that there will be objections from the prospects. Every communicator must be prepared to overcome these objections at any time during the entire course of the conversation. There are, however, occasions when probing reveals that there is little likelihood of converting the prospect to a customer, and it should be stressed to the communicators that it is far cheaper on those occasions to thank the person at the other end of the receiver for their time and politely end the call.

What's in it for the prospect

It must be borne in mind that the prospect is only interested in the benefit to himself or to his company if he proceeds to buy your product.

The following case history used this premise very successfully.

The object of the exercise was to induce stationery retailers to sell a particular brand of typewriter. The form given to the interviewer is shown in Figure 9.

As a result of this telephone sales campaign 1000 retailers were contacted at a total cost of £3500. Of these 206 agreed to make firm timed appointments to see the representative with a view to consider stocking the typewriters.

Figure 9 Sample script

(At first contact) 'Good morning/afternoon. May I please have the name of your managing director/buyer?'

Name and initials _____

Position _____

(On connection) 'Good morning/afternoon, Mr (contact name). My name is Tom Jones and I am calling on behalf of the Customer Services Division of XYZ Typewriter Co.'

1 'Do you sell typewriters from your premises?' (yes/no)
(If 'yes', continue)
(If 'no') 'well, I am surprised you don't sell typewriters, but I understand you do sell office equipment and stationery products. That's correct, isn't it?'

2 *(After response, continue)* 'If we could show you a way to sell typewriters profitably I am sure that you would be interested.'
Pause for comment

---

3 'As you may be aware, Mr (contact name), from surveys taken within our industry, XYZ Typewriter Company will sell one out of every four typewriters sold in the UK this year. And on top of that, six out of every ten electric compacts and portables sold are sold by XYZ Typewriter Company. So obviously, if you aren't currently stocking XYZ typewriters, you are missing a great profit opportunity.

'Later this month, we're starting a major national advertising and promotion campaign costing over £500,000 which is going to prove very proftable to you if you participate. Mr Green, our Area Manager, has asked me to call you personally as he has not yet had the chance to meet you and explain the advantages to you of this vast campaign. He is in your area next *(day 1)* and *(day2)* and has asked me to call you to check which of these days would be more suitable for you to meet him.

'Do you have your diary in front of you?'

'Which would you prefer, Mr (contact name)? (day 1) or (day 2)?

Appt. _____ Day _____ Date _____ Month _____ Time _____

(Repeat) 'So that is (time) o'clock, on (day) of (month). Now, just to make sure that Mr Green brings along the relevant information on the promotion for your particular business, may I just ask you some brief questions?'

Q1: If they sell XYZ typewriters at present, ask 'Who is your current wholesaler?'

Q2: 'Which typewriters do you sell at present?'
(manufacturers)

1 _____
2 _____
3 _____
4 _____
5 _____

Phrases that make phoneselling easier

Simple phrases can make all the difference in detailing benefits and features. Here are some of the best:

Because it has ....
And this will give you ....
I'd like personally to tell you about ....
Not only ... but also ....
Even though ... we can still offer you ....
Additionally ....
Incredibly, we can still maintain ....

Closing a sale over the phone

There are four different ways of closing a sale:

1 *Direct*: 'May I confirm your name and address so that the order will be delivered *correctly*?'

2 *Assumptive*: 'Did you want three white shirts, Mr Brown, or have you decided to take three of the blue as well?'

3 *Optional*: 'Could Mr Green call on Monday at around 10 o'clock, or would you prefer to see him on another day? Perhaps Wednesday or Thursday?'

4 *Deferred*: 'I'm grateful for your interest and time, Mr Brown. Which day would you like me to call back so that you can confirm your order?'

It is important to develop techniques of knowing exactly when to close a presentation and to recognize the buying signals. It is a matter of listening very carefully to what is being said at the other end of the telephone.

Here are some examples of responses which are signalling that it is the correct time to close:

1 When the prospect responds by showing interest in your presentation:

It is time we thought about a microcomputer.... Our systems are rather out-of-date....
It is time we looked at our policies again....

2 If the prospect asks questions:

Do you have it in different colours?
What are the terms of payment?
Are there any leasing arrangements?

The script shown in Figure 10 was used in approaching housewives with the object of their becoming agents for a mail order company:

As a result of this campaign a very encouraging 10 per cent of those receiving 'cold calls' expressed an interest in becoming agents.

Figure 10 Sample script

'Good morning/Evening, Ms Smith. This is Pamela Jones of XYZ Mail Order.'

1 'Have you seen any of our recent advertising? (yes/no)
(If 'yes', go to Question 2)
(If 'no') 'Well, as you probably know, we are a reputable and long-established catalogue mail order company, and we advertise in the national papers and women's magazines.'

2 'May I ask if you have any knowledge of mail order?' (yes/no)
(If 'no', go to Question 3)
(If 'yes') 'Do you actually run a catalogue? Have you thought of applying for a copy of ours?' (yes/no)
(If 'yes' go to question 4)
(If 'no' go to question 3)'

3 'I am sure you would be interested in knowing a little more about how profitable the XYZ Mail Order Catalogue could be for you.'
(Pause for comment)
'Apart from the convenience of mail order fashion shopping, the credit facilities and the fact that you get 10 per cent commission on everything you sell and of course buy for yourself means a *welcome extra income for you*, of course. Some of our agents earned as much as £800 in two months before Christmas, as well as getting a regular income throughout the year.'

4 'If you think you might be interested in running a catalogue, may I just ask if you are over 18 years of age?'
(If 'yes' go to question 5)
(If 'no') 'Do you have any friends or relatives who are over 18 and might be interested in having a catalogue? Then you could choose goods from the catalogue too.' (yes/no)
(If under 18) 'I'm sorry, we can't appoint an agent who is under 18, but I hope you will contact us when you reach 18. Thank you very much for your time, Ms Smith. Goodnight.

5 'May I ask your local XYZ mail order representative to call with a copy of the catalogue for you to see?' (yes/no)
(If 'yes') 'What is the most convenient time for you? Thank you very much for your time, Mrs Smith. Your local representative will be in touch with you in the next few days. Goodnight.'
(If 'no') 'We can arrange to send a catalogue and application form by post if you prefer, but usually we find that people who are thinking of becoming an XYZ agent find it very helpful to chat with their local representative, who can answer any queries you may have and offer some useful advice on how to run an agency successfully.'
(If still 'no') 'Very well, Mrs Smith, we'll be very happy to put a

catalogue and application form in the post to you, together with a leaflet which explains some of the benefits you could enjoy as an XYZ agent. Thank you very much for your time. Goodnight.'

Overcoming resistance

A good communicator will not need to be a Sherlock Holmes in order to spot and interpret the clues he gets. Any of the following responses are a sure sign of resistance to the product or service being offered:

1. *Negative comments*

'I've never liked that firm.'
'It's too big to fit on my desk.'
'I've had one before and it was no good.'
'Can't see the need for one.'
'Much too expensive.'

2 *Silence*

No response to any pauses.

3 *Lack of interest*

'Oh yes!'
'Maybe.'
'Perhaps'
'If you say so.'
'All right...OK....Uh-huh...etc., etc.'

4 *Doubts*

'I wouldn't have thought so.'
'Do you *really* believe that?'
'I don't agree.'

5 *Dissembling*

'Call me back another time.'
'I'll have to ask my wife/husband/boss, etc.'
'I must think about it.'

Whilst recognition of actual resistance is quickly learned, it is more difficult to gauge how to identify the real underlying reasons for the prospect's resistance. Until you do this, you will not be able to sell to him or her.

The way to throw light on the hidden reasons for the objection is to ask questions – in fact, to go back to the technique of *probing*. Good opening phrases following resistance are:

- 'The special features of this are of course obvious to a man in your position, Mr Brown.'
- 'You do understand all the advantages, such as A, B, and C, don't you, Mr Brown?'

This will give Mr Brown the chance to talk a little more, and for the communicator to have an opportunity of realizing and overcoming the many obstacles.

Resolving resistance

1 A cash flow problem.

Solve the problem
We can offer you a very low rate over a 3–5 five year period.

2 We don't need a telex machine. We only send one message a day, and use a local bureau.

Open new ideas
Our new model will enable you to have the message sent at night at the lowest rates and you will probably find that it will be cheaper and faster to have the convenience of your own telex.

3 I understand your service department is really slow and very expensive.

Give proof
In the last six years we have sold 20,000 microwaves and have only had 200 service calls. 150 of these were made within 24 hours without any charge to the consumer.

4 32K is much too small I'm told for my accounting needs.

Redirect attention
Our new accounting programme is better than anything else available on the

market and used by many of your competitors.

Deny strongly

5 I expect you charge for every single extra that you can: deliveries and so forth.

No Mr Brown: XYZ make it a policy to have no 'hidden costs' at all.

Third party referral

6 Everybody in the trade seems to order from your competitors, the ABC Company.

By no means, Mr Brown. Hardings, a *very* successful company as you know, only order from us and in fact have doubled up on last year.

Always bear in mind that resistance does not necessarily crop up in the middle or the end of a presentation. Resistance can be there from the very inception of the call.

As an example, the prospect could say, 'XYZ Company? No thank you, I've had very poor service from you in the past.' This of course is an example of resistance which must be overcome before the presentation carries on.

Always set a call plan beforehand in conjunction with the script and provide the communicators with ancillary material and details of the reasons why your products or services are better than anything else available.

Before commencing a new script, ensure that a full briefing takes place and the key words are noted. These will always include the benefits to the prospect as well as other advantageous features. The value and strength of the key words and phrases must be emphasized to the communicators – as well as the dangers of omitting them from the 'sales pitch'.

9

Incoming calls

As recently as three years ago, filling out and posting off a coupon was the only direct response way of applying for mail order goods, brochures, information packs and booking theatre tickets. The situation completely altered with the wide distribution of credit cards, and the use of TV advertisements to promote *incoming* telephone numbers. Organizations such as Teledata with their 200-0-200 numbers were amongst the first in this field, and British Telecom themselves were soon to realize the potential of this type of business, and opened their own Incoming Call company in Bristol.

Most consumers do not have any objection to writing off for something which has caught their interest. By the time, however, that they have torn the advertisement out of the publication, found a pen, filled in the coupon, acquired an envelope and a stamp, and remembered to drop it into the letterbox, many of them will have become distracted from their original purchasing purpose. Often too, lethargy or lack of time means that the envelope never gets addressed, let alone actually posted. The coupons which have been cut out are put aside for attention at a later date – and then forgotten. Picked up again after a few days have lapsed, they are often discarded, because the earlier enthusiasm isn't there any more.

Organizations who use telephone numbers in their advertisements, side by side with the usual name and address panel, find that they can receive up to *one and a half times more response* from phone enquiries than they do from the post. Conversions too are usually higher. The time lapse between making a call and receiving a brochure is much shorter than posting a coupon and waiting for a response. Indeed, the use of the phone speeds up everything and boosts sales and cash flow dramatically. An oft-quoted saying in the direct mail business is, 'The first brochure in your hand is the one you are most likely to purchase from.' That's true enough – as the holiday tour operators well know – and by using the telephone to make their requests consumers receive their brochures that much quicker. An added plus for the advertiser is that once having achieved a voice-to-voice contact, the prospect is now much more aware of the company's existence and a pleasant reception from the voice at the other end of the phone is an added inducement when considering his purchase.

Incoming telephone call training is as equally important at outgoing. The incoming telephone communicator is a shop window for the company, either enticing the customer to come in and buy the goods, or putting up a barrier and providing reasons for the prospect to go elsewhere. Wanting the business is just not enough: pleasant and enthusiastic communicators trained to sell and to communicate the merchandise or service being offered by painting 'word pictures' are essential.

An incoming call communicator should not be just an 'order taker' but a trained salesperson who is fully conversant with stock positions, and the relative advantages of the items being sold. In exactly the same way as an outgoing call communicator, the incoming sales person must be able quickly and picturesquely to describe the benefits to the *prospect* rather than to the company doing the selling.

Freephone

Although quite expensive for the advertiser, Freephone, is used effectively by many organizations. Mercedes Benz, for example, uses it in promoting their truck division. Transport managers and interested prospects may ring the operator anywhere in Britain and by quoting Freephone Mercedes Benz be put in touch with a member of the company who provides immediate comprehensive information on the company's vehicles, and also arranges for a test drive at any appropriate dealer location. One of the advantages of Freephone is that it can be set up very quickly, and there is no need to make any commitment to a long-term contract.

RCF

An alternative to the Freephone system is the remote call forwarding service – RCF. This allows you to use local telephone numbers in any town in the country, and have the calls routed to your centre of operations. Consumers are often hesitant to make outside area calls because of the cost (and who can blame them) and this can seriously inhibit the effectiveness of a telephone direct response programme. If, however, the telephone number is a local one, the number of calls should increase substantially. Once the appropriate number has been dialled, the caller is answered with a recorded message explaining that they will be shortly connected with the advertiser. Of course whilst the caller pays local charges only, the recipient pays for the STD part.

The main advantage of RCF is that it is both quick and easy to obtain, and enables the subscriber to have a telephone presence in locations away from its offices.

DSN

In the USA, the 800 service, in which the recipient pays for the call entirely, is thought to increase the response rate by about 40 per cent. The speed and ease of dialling directly without going through the operator must be an attraction for those in a hurry (which is most of the working population).

With DSN imminent in the UK, it will probably be accepted to use this facility in most forms of advertising. By dialling a special national number beginning '0800' the caller can be connected automatically to the answering centre.

The DSN service will be divisible into up to eight geographical areas. A single DSN telephone number can have national coverage or be available to just a limited number of areas. Using a single national DSN telephone number, calls may be routed to destinations in each of the eight areas.

Having said all this, however, I do stress again the need for constant training and evaluation of those communicators who will be answering the calls before setting up and taking advantage of the services available.

Incoming call success stories

The range of marketing and service activities that are now encouraging incoming calls is really remarkable, and there is

every sign that the tendency will not only continue, but there is
every sign that the tendency will not only continue, but increase.

Financial information

Financial services worth millions of pounds have been
developed in great measure by the incoming call services of the
unit trust companies and insurance brokers in which subscribers
are invited to phone-in for the latest available investment know
how. Often as many as 500 callers during a weekend will listen
to up to three minutes of taped information, and in one particular instance a regular average 10 per cent of the callers invite
contact by leaving their name and address.

Brochure requests

A tour operator regularly running annual direct response advertisements decided to include a specific telephone number
inviting prospective customers to phone in for a brochure, as an
alternative to posting a coupon. Following the first two inser-
tions, the company received 2000 requests by telephone and
1400 by mail. The first interesting point which ultimately
emerged was that the conversion rate from the telephoned
enquiries was 7 per cent higher than from the written requests.
The reason for this was easy to isolate. Those telephoning
received their brochure within 48 hours and the initial interest
in the enquiry was stimulated with the result that bookings were
made. Those people sending in the original application by mail
had to wait between five and seven days before the brochure was
in their hands. The second point is that the tour operator
benefited with a better cash flow. Bookings – and deposits –
from the telephone were received that much quicker.

Dealer location service

One of the complaints received from the authorized dealers of
one of the divisions of this large automobile company importing
cars from Europe was that they were unable to (i) make easy
contact with the company as telephone lines were often engaged
and personnel unavailable or engaged on other job functions;
and (ii) valuable time was lost in trying to locate specific models.

The solution was to set up a dealer location incoming call
service using an outside bureau. This had the advantage of

immediately highlighting this separate service, and also of ensuring that there were always staff available to answer these specific enquiries.

The bureau were provided daily with a computer print-out of every model and its location, and thousands of calls from dealers were handled pleasantly and immediately. The efficiency of the operation was reflected in the change of the dealers' attitude towards the company's marketing – with higher sales resulting.

Consumer retail location service

In order to encourage consumers to use their carpet cleaning product, the manufacturer ran a series of direct response advertisements using only a coupon with a telephone number. Prospective users were invited to telephone and find out the name of their nearest stockists. They were asked to indicate their favourite shopping areas, and the incoming call communicators were then able to indicate the nearest of stockist in that specific location.

The promotion was very successful in terms of direct sales, encouraging the retail stockists who appreciated the manufacturer's support and enhancing consumer goodwill.

Planning an incoming call service

All too often incoming telephone numbers are advertised which create very little appeal or incentive for the prospect to call right away. 'Ring for your brochure' is fine, but a stronger approach would encourage the prospect to action: for example, 'Ring for your brochure before 3 o'clock and we promise to put it in the post to you 1st Class the same day.' Or even 'Ring for your brochure this week: post back a completed booking form to us and we'll arrange to send you a pocket camera or ....' Why not? It is an excepted fact of direct response that mailing with an incentive will often outpull a straight offer. The same creative planning should be used for incoming call generation.

Testing the incoming call system is totally unheard of at the moment. But there is no better way of projecting likely response than by testing on a particular conurbation, or approach, so that the amount of likely callers may be realistically assessed and the correct number of telephone lines made available. On the current hit-and-miss attitude of many advertisers, the situation often arises where advertised telephone lines are permanently engaged to the frustration of the caller, and the detriment of the campaign, or a large number of idle manned telephones have been needlessly booked and paid for.

Transcription

The one flaw in this system is the transcription – a problem when calls are taken 'live', even more when answering machines are used. To minimize this the operators responsible for obtaining the information as well as supervisors must have an adequate knowledge of each town and county and be taught the essential need for (i) clear handwriting; and (ii) insistence on obtaining the postal code, which is often the main clue to the true location of the enquirer.

Transcription can be data prepped straight into the computer: always be aware of course that any problems by way of faulty disks or tapes may mean that the information is completely lost. Time and effort saved is considerable and could mean that an address label is generated within minutes of the original call.

10

Computerization and telephone marketing

With the advancement in telecommunications and the emergence of telephone marketing as one of the fastest growing media in Europe, a combination of techniques using the most innovative office automation will always be an essential part of the continuous growth pattern.

Telephone marketing can, if handled manually bring with it a continuous problem of a surfeit of paper. Scripts, reports, information cards, telephone number files – all of these add up to a vast accumulation in the course of just one week. A well-equipped operation will therefore be linked to a central computer with either an individual station for every communicator, or one at the end of each line or team unit. Here will be stored the customer data base, telephone numbers and, where relevant, details of previous orders or particular requirements.

At this stage the decision must be made as to whether the communicators purely write out the information for later entry by the data-prep personnel, or whether they are trained to enter response directly. The latter is more systematic but has two major problems. One is the obvious fact that fewer contacts will be made unless the operator is particularly proficient at data prep, and the other, more serious drawback, is that a good communicator cannot always necessarily be taught to efficiently data-prep, and of course vice versa.

In the event that you are able to train telephone communicator personnel to data-prep, it is necessary to ensure that adequate and comfortable headphones are provided so that both hands are free. Headphones are, as a general rule, not very acceptable to communicators; they often complain of discomfort, hair tangling and earache, and it is worth experimenting with whatever is currently available in the marketplace, ensuring that your supervisor and staff are consulted and involved before the type and model are finally chosen.

Telephone marketing is a modern media. Technology is improving daily and we are of course only at the very edge of the developments. During recent space shuttle missions a special 900 number was made available so that the public could call and listen to the astronauts' conversations with each other and with the ground base. Each caller paid $0.50 for the 3 minute privilege, which was then added to their phone bill in the usual way.

Integration of voice and data

Incoming call divisions need constantly to enhance productivity in order continually to boost profits. Systems have been developed which will allow the communicator to receive an enquiry and immediately retrieve the information sought and have it displayed on a computer screen.

Should the enquirer be, for example, one of the sales reps, it is possible to transmit a copy of the information directly onto his personal computer screen.

Most systems include a liquid crystal display (LCD) panel which guides the user through each step in plain language. Run by interactive software, the display presents the commands that are required at each point in a call. The user need only push the correct soft key to continue the call progressively. Some programmes wisely include a 'help' button which assists new operators to become proficient in a much shorter time than previously had to be allowed.

Incidentally, in the event of a second incoming call whilst the first is in progress, it is possible to 'hold' the original enquirer in order to briefly connect and ask the second caller to hold the line.

The increased communications efficiency achieved by a company for a company dependent upon integrating its telephone answering with data computerized systems justifies the outlay and provides an immediate and informative service, ensuring maximum usage of each working hour.

Computer telephones

It was inevitable that, with the swift and overwhelmingly fast rise of the computer in every sphere from business to consumer, computer telephones would swiftly find a place in the scheme of things.

Computerized telephones, which have been in operation in the USA for several years, have had a very difficult history. Viewed at first with suspicion their use was outlawed in several states, including California, but gradually they have become accepted as a valuable aid in telephone marketing campaigns everywhere. Available equipment is quite extensive ranging from machines manufactured for the larger organization which allows for thousands of outgoing or incoming calls to be made during a short period, to the very simple unsophisticated machines, which cost around £6000 to buy and can be simply programmed to telephone at specific hours. Instead of the usual telephone marketing room with its booths, or carefully placed tables, with a buzzing sound from the communicators, and a supervisor gliding from person to person, visualize a small room with rows of computer telephones, each with a printer attached churning out printouts that measure productivity and provide continuous and unending call reports.

Computerized telephone marketing does not have any mystique. You can decide exactly who to sell to, and at which particular time. The programme can be organized so that you achieve exactly the correct amount of 'leads' you need.

In my firm we intend to use the Computer machines ourselves as ancillary back-up to our Phonesell division where the information we need to impart may be directed very simply. For example, a computer telephone is an excellent instrument for simple research. The method allows for an impartial approach to the person being interviewed. Its attitude, and therefore the response, does not alter through being tired, irritable or – the big problem of telephone marketing – bored with asking the same questions continuously. Because the voice of the questioner is always pleasant and bright, the replies to a computerized questionnaire are often better in terms of a more enthusiastic, interested response.

The answers are taped and a print-out of telephone numbers automatically emitted proves the 'honesty' of the research which may be invaluable in those cases where perhaps a particularly important issue is being debated.

In the USA, computer telephones were used extensively prior

to the elections. Millions of homes received a call from a 'live' operator introducing the party being represented and then stating that the presidential candidate would like to talk to the respondent for just 60 seconds. Very few people would refuse such a call, and the presidential candidate's message was relayed into each home in a very dramatic, and certainly effective, manner.

In the same way, the system can enhance any campaign by using a pre-recorded message from a well-known voice. After all, how many of us would refuse to listen to Margaret Thatcher telling us to vote for the Tories or Prince Charles asking us to contribute to the World Wildlife Fund?

Computer telephones can be used by themselves or with a 'live' operator who makes the initial introduction and ensures contact with the correct prospect − because this is one of the functions that the computer telephone cannot perform.

Voice sensitive, it will react to a response by continuing the conversation when the person answering ceases talking, and therefore the script has to be very carefully thought out on a totally different basis from the normal telephone concept. There is no use starting off by saying 'May I speak to the lady of the house?' because the response could be 'I am the lady of the house' or 'She is out' or even 'There is no lady of the house!' The computer telephone would of course continue the conversation irrespective of the contents of the response.

However, many sales messages can be relayed successfully by thinking out the format very carefully. A taped conversation could read like this for example.

Good evening, this is a computer talking on behalf of the new Hamburger Bar which has just opened in XYZ High Street. We particularly want to meet as many of our neighbours as we can. So this is an invitation to you and your family and friends to come along for a meal any evening right up until 11pm. As a gesture of our neighbourly feelings there will be a bottle of wine waiting for you. Or, of course, if you're under age or don't drink spirits, we will be pleased to provide some minerals. May we expect you soon?.

After a pause for a yes/no response, the computer would complete the call by saying 'Thank you for your time neighbour. Good night.'

Similar localized campaigns have produced a high response resulting in completely filled seats for a restaurant chain. The computer phone can either be activated by pre-punched individual numbers, or for a localized promotion it can be provided with the first digits of a particular exchange and then programmed to dial sequential numbers automatically without any further data preparation. The Computer will dial each number three times at set intervals in the event that there is not any response from the first call. This latter facility is one which is causing a great deal of concern to the responsible telephone marketing industry who feel that random or sequential dialling should not be undertaken. My own company heavily underlines this sentiment.

Computer telephones are a particular source of worry to many people because of the possibility of mis-use and it is hoped that the manufacturers of the equipment will continue to market the machines responsibly.

The story is told in America of a frustrated car salesman who had spent a long time with a customer ostensibly wishing to purchase a deluxe Cadillac. Trial car rides were organized; the prospect's wife chose the particular colour scheme and a trade-in price was agreed for the existing family car. However, the prospect could not make up his mind and the salesman was driven to biting his finger nails over the 'on/off' situation with the possibility of a very substantial commission at risk. It got to the stage when the prospect promised to put his signature to the order form within the next 24 hours, and the salesman, due to go on holiday that day, delayed his plans in order to finalize the deal. You guessed it! The prospect didn't sign. The frustrated car salesman then rented time from a computer-phone bureau and set the machine to phone the prospect at 30 minute intervals for a 24-hour period starting at 1 am. The terrible strategy worked. After the twelfth call, the prospect cracked, and he was only too happy to contact the showroom at 9 am and beg them to bring the contract around for signing.

One can visualize the same application by other less scrupulous salesmen in the car, double glazing and central heating fields, to name but a few industries, and trust that stringent safeguards will continue to be applied.

Another use of the machine in the USA is for checking out on truancy in the schools. One state has dramatically reduced its truancy record by programming the Computer phone with the telephone numbers of all pupils who had been consistently absent. The number of absences recorded were in fact so great that it would have been impossible for the officers personally to visit. The use of the system has reduced the state truancy tangibly and the idea is now being considered by many other educational authorities.

Computer telephone techniques have been developed which, rather than endeavouring to intimate to the prospect that they are speaking to a 'live' operator, emphasize the fact that it is a computer and, by its novelty, encourage the recipient to take part in what is in all probability their first call of this kind.

The most successful technique is to commence with a greeting followed by the words: 'This is a computer talking to you on behalf of XYZ....' A pleasant memory in the minds of the prospects can be achieved by completing the call by saying 'Thank you so much for your time. To a computer you sounded a really nice human....'

Although basically more successful in consumer promotions, a computer phone can be used in the commercial world cost-effectively to update mailing lists; find out the names applicable to specific job titles, and to sell directly to one-man businesses or in any situation where the decision maker is most likely to answer the telephone.

I do think however that the area of incoming calls is where the computer telephone really scores. In those circumstances where the only purpose of answering a telephone 'live' is either to impart a specific piece of information or to obtain particulars in order to send a brochure, or a combination of both, the computer telephone can undertake the job more accurately than a human. After all the answers are on tape and can be verified if there is any doubt at all about the prospect's requirements.

The cost of using a computer telephone is considerably less than a 'live' operator and therefore, providing one bears in mind that there are definite limitations on its usage, there is adequate reason to use this system.

Cost

Used as an answering mode for brochure responses, one would expect a three-hour shift to compare like this:

Based on two telephones:

Live	*Computer telephone*
2 personnel @ £4.00 per hour = £24.00	2 machine time @ £5.00 per hour = £30.00
Supervisor @ £5.00 per hour = £15.00	
Data prep or typing of say 100 enquiries £12.00	Transcription £15.00
Cost: 5.1p per enquiry	Cost: 4.5p per enquiry

A further advantage is of course that irrespective of weather conditions, health and other circumstances the machines would be operational.

Outgoing call costs can also be cut through using the computer and one would expect the computer telephone to make more diallings than an operator.

As an example, let us consider a repeat telephone campaign to small drapery shops inviting them to stock up with their regular brand of ladies tights. Because this is undertaken every four weeks, it is known that there will be an order taken on a ratio of 3:1.

Based on a 7-hour day (9am-5pm excluding the lunch hour) on one telephone this is an actual comparison:

'Live' operator		*Computer*	
Diallings	175	Diallings	210
Actual contacts	60	Actual contacts	70
Orders on ratio of 3:1	20	Orders on ratio of 3.18:1	22
Operator at £4.00 per hour	28.00	Machine @ £5.00 per hour	35.00
Supervisor at £5.00 per hour	35.00	Cost of 400 units @ 4.5p	18.00
Cost of 350 units @ 4.5p	15.75	Transcription @ 15p	10.50
	£78.75		£63.50
Cost per order = 3.93p		Cost per order = 2.89p	

You will note that the computer is able to make a greater amount of diallings (no visits to the toilet, sneezing or fatigue at the end of a long day), but the ratio of orders to contact is slightly less. However, all telephone marketing is a numbers game and the increased number of diallings produces sufficient extra orders to maintain a lower cost-per-order obtained.

Call logging

A very valuable asset in any telephone marketing department is a call logging system which monitors each dialling and produces:

Date and time call is made;
The telephone number digits dialled;
Duration of the call (in minutes)
Length of time taken to answer; and
Whether the call is incoming or outgoing.

Whilst invaluable in terms of costing each operation, the system can also be used by an able telephone marketing manager to pinpoint those of his staff who are not dialling in sufficient numbers or those who perhaps are making out-of-area calls without authority. But, most importantly, it will also show clearly where the length of call being made is not justified in terms of results.

One of the very hardest maxims to learn is: 'If the person at the other end of the phone is clearly *not* a prospect, thank them for their time and finish the conversation.'

The logging system when compared with the actual sales or results achieved will enable the telephone marketing manager effectively to tighten-up his operation.

This is particularly helpful in terms of an in-coming call facility when one can see at a glance how long it took for the operator to answer each call and at the same time evaluate the exact number of enquiries received.

The equipment is sold by quite a few manufacturers in the UK and used extensively particularly in the hotel industry where they have need to charge back calls accurately onto clients' accounts.

Computer software for telemarketing

Three American manufacturers have pioneered software for telephone marketing. A main area of sales has been the Fortune 1000 companies. As an indication of the growth and respect for this media in the USA, AT & T reports that during 1983 US companies spent $13.6 billion on telephone marketing phone calls and equipment – phones, lines, computers. And *Fortune* estimated telephone sales of goods and services at $75 billion annually. Although figures are not as yet available from BT, I believe that the UK will rapidly follow this trend.

Early, Cloud & Co of Rhode Island has developed state-of-the-art software to support inbound and outbound telephone marketing on any Wang VS equipment. The system has the ability for end-users to create their own telephone marketing scripts and has a high degree of menu response for ease of usage in view of the fact that communicators are unlikely to be trained DP operators. Benefits of computerized software include:

Script control processor. This ensures that communicators never need to pause and wait while conversing with prospects.

Data formating. This provides for the possibility of receiving and sending to outside systems for validation.

Dynamic loading. Highlighting key points of campaign ensuring higher sales closing ratios.

Script builder. Allows non DP staff the opportunity to generate scripts in a shorter time and provides for communicator to enhance where circumstances allow for this.

Disposition codes. The system maintains all statistical information.

Real time activity monitor. Provides capability to monitor individual operator applications, campaigns and office performance. Aids and quickens supervisory functions.

Many other functions are available in using this sytem, which does not come cheaply, but certainly covers all features of a successful operation.

Telephone marketing is unique in that it does not simply decrease sales costs, but also increases revenues. The merger of the telephone and data processing technologies is an invaluable tool for achieving success.

11

The winning combination

Telephone marketing can stand on its own merits when combined with direct mail, but in certain circumstances doing so produces really startling results. The trick is to put together a 'winning combination', one which can increase the value of both media, dramatically and cost-effectively.

This chapter tells you how to go about it.

The winning formula works in a variety of situations, but it is most obviously successful in 'cold calls' – especially when these factors are involved:

- the name and address of your file is an unknown quantity;
- your own company is not a household name;
- your introducing a brand-new product or service to the market;
- you're unsure which person within your prospect's company is the decision-maker;
- you're offering a high-value product or service for sale;
- your product needs detailed explanation – as, for example, for a piece of technical equipment;
- your product's or service's appeal is limited to certain periods of the year, or depends on contractual or other arrangements; and
- your market is very precisely defined – possibly consisting only of organizations within certain classifications, having specific turnovers, or a particular number of personnel.

If your marketing situation fits any – or several – of these criteria, then a combined direct mail and Phonesell operation can be of major help. But which comes first, the chicken or the egg? The telephoning or the direct mail?

The answer to that depends first of all on how accurate your mailing list is, and whether it is made up of larger firms or owner/manager businesses. If the latter is the case – for example, if you have an accurate current list of 25,000 confectioners/tobacconists/newsagents (CTNs) and you intend to exclude multiples – then the first step in your two-stage campaign might well be a mailing. That's because you can be secure in the knowledge that it will almost certainly be the decision-maker who opens your envelope and reads your mailing piece.

Let's take the case of a well-known confectionery manufacturer whom we'll call 'Jones'. Each year, that company faces the same problem – that of making sure it has produced enough Easter eggs to meet the anticipated demand but having no stock remaining on its shelves after Easter Monday. The Jones Company needs to create a demand which can be filled by the 500 wholesalers who already stock its merchandise – and it needs to do this in good time if accurate production is to be planned.

It solved its problem in this way:

An attractive 'pop-up' mailing piece was sent out in the second week of January. This offered the 25,000 CTNs (i) an incentive in the form of an opportunity to enter an exciting holiday competition when they placed an order for the Jones Easter Eggs and (ii) attractive mobile window display materials.

A covering letter contained a list of the wholesalers stocking the product, categorized by area, and asked the CTN to phone-in if his own particular supplier was not on this list. All direct accounts were excluded from this promotion and eliminated from the mailing.

Research showed that the Jones Company's mailing piece – packaged attractively and detailing the Incentive Holiday Scheme – was received enthusiastically by the CTN retailers. Moreover 1381 CTNs telephoned to say their usual wholesalers were not on Jones's list. This information gave Jones's sales force the opportunity to visit those wholesalers and convert them into becoming customers, by *proving* that a real demand for Jones's Easter eggs existed in the retail trade.

By February 1st, 3612 CTN's had entered Jones's holiday competition – proving they had actually placed orders with their wholesalers. These 3612, together with the 1381 who had made incoming calls, were then eliminated from the master

Figure 11 Sample script

Introduction
Good morning/afternoon, my name is . . . ., and I'm calling on behalf of Jones's Confectionery Co. Are you the owner or manager, sir,/madam?

(Owner/Manager)

May I have your name plaese? _____

With only a few weeks before the Easter Egg rush, we want to make sure you acted on the mailing piece we sent a couple of weeks ago. You do remember the leaflet with the pop-up, don't you Mr/Mrs . . . .?   yes/no

a *If yes:*
Have you placed your order yet for Jones's Bunny Easter Egg, Mr/Mrs . . . .?   yes/no

If no:
The Jones range of Easter Eggs is going to be very heavily advertised on TV, Mr/Mrs . . . . Retail prices range from 50p to £5 and each egg is colourfully packaged with attractive red and blue ribbons, and the more expensive have satin-lined boxes. The hollow eggs are a new recipe milk chocolate and the filled eggs contain our best-selling Golden Assortment. If you give me the name of your usual distributor, Mr/Mrs . . . ., I will make sure he has sufficient stock, or else I will call you back with the name of your nearest stockist. Who is your usual wholesaler, Mr/Mrs . . .?

What sort of price range do you usually buy? The smaller eggs are in outers of 12 and the larger ones are in cartons of 3s.

_____ outers of 12

_____ outers of 3

Objections	*Response*
Already placed order for other products/I've spent too much/Easter egg business is declining	I do recommend you include Bunnies in your stock. We have two-minute spot ads in peak viewing times and this always makes demand heavy. We can also arrange attract window and counter display material.
I'd like to see what they look like.	I'll put another leaflet in the post to you today, Mr/Mrs . . . . Thank for time, etc.

promotional file; the rest were telephoned over a two-week period, using the script shown in Figure 11.

This promotion produced an immediate response of a further 712 definite orders. This meant not only a successful launch of the product, but a total sell-out for the manufacturer.

When the telephone call is the first stage

The Easter egg promotion is an example of one in which the mailing piece should *precede* the telephone call.

But, however good your file of prospect names and addresses may be, there are many instances when the telephone call should cost-effectively precede the mailing, instead of the other way around.

Take the case of a Timeshare operation. Here, the company produced a very colourful brochure and attendant literature, which cost approximately £1.50, posted to a UK address. Media coupon advertising had brought in a very fair response, but conversions following the mailing out of the information package continued to be low.

A telephone questionnaire was undertaken. This showed that while the content of the package was attractive, the respondents to the coupon advertising campaign were, in the main, not really prospective timeshare buyers for a variety of reasons, such as age, holiday requirements, numbers in the family, and so forth.

Before proceeding to mail out any more brochures, the company organized a telephone follow-up call to those prospects who had sent in coupons. Each was thanked for having expressed interest, and gently probed to see if they could be converted into becoming subscribers to the scheme. Of those sending in coupons 23 per cent were discounted in this way, at a saving of £1.50 per name and address, of the remainder 40 per cent responded with further interest when the courteous call was followed up by the company's informative, albeit expensive, mailing piece.

We have used the same two-stage technique cost-effectively for a wide variety of merchandise and services. One case involved a developer and his agent who were trying to rent out shops in a new precinct. They were spending considerable sums of money on advertising the available space in the press, on TV and radio, via direct mail. Due to various factors, the shops moved very slowly and the leases became a serious problem.

The developer produced a list of his ideal tenants, covering every kind of retail outlet, as well as ancillary services such as cleaners, shoe repairers, launderettes, and so forth.

A telephone call was made to every outlet of these types in a radius of two miles of the shopping precinct. The object was to speak to the decision-maker (and, in the case of multiples, to find out the names and addresses of people in authority) to determine whether there was possible interest in the leases being offered.

Of those contacted 11 per cent indicated that they might consider a shop in the new precinct, and each of these was mailed a brochure and a personalized letter. This gave details of viewing times, rents, length of leases being offered, and all other relevant information.

Of the people who were mailed this material 40 per cent later actually contacted the developer's agents. 229 viewed the property and a sizeable number of the leases were disposed of, at an overall cost to the developer of just £6000.

Another example of the same formula concerns a large paper group which wished to introduce into the marketplace a new hand-drying machine using their own paper products.

An excellent sales force had tried repeatedly to make inroads into larger industrial and commercial premises, but without much success. The main stumbling block was that it proved very difficult to pinpoint who was the individual company's decision-maker responsible for purchasing washroom equipment, and even more difficult to contact the person who could influence such an order.

Media advertising and direct mail brought insufficient response to provide enough 'leads' and it was therefore decided to telephone 11,000 companies who fitted certain parameters, such as size. The companies were told the purpose of the call and the questionnaire looked like the one shown in Figure 12.

It was found, in the main, that the switchboard operators of the contacted companies were able and willing to provide the necessary answers; as a result, 8700 questionnaires were fully completed. One interesting and important fact which emerged

Figure 12 Questionnaire

Name of company ___ Head office ___ No. of staff in building _____

Address _____ Tel _____

No. of toilets:

Male _____ Female _____

Purchasing officer(s) _____

(1) Current hand drying methods _____

(2) Are they satisfactory? _____

Executive director _____

Managing director's P/A Secretary _____

Personnel Welfare Officer _____

---

was that it was the managing director's *personal secretary* who often was the most influential in making such decisions.

A personalized mailing was then sent to the 23,000 individual names and addresses at the 8700 firms. Salesmen were given carbon copies of the letters, together with the information sheets, and they were then able to visit every outlet, knowing who would be in a position to place an order, who would influence such a decision, what the opposition was – and if equipment currently in use was satisfactory.

This promotion helped to successfully launch the product.

Phone-mail-phone combinations

In 25 years in direct mail marketing, the question I am asked most frequently is, 'What is the *minimum* response I can expect from my mailing campaign?'

It is a question which is impossible to answer, because it depends on so many factors such as lists, mailing pieces, timing, pricing, appeal and, of course, the need for the product or service being offered. Yet a three-stage approach can guarantee a success rate because of the very nature of the promotion itself. Here's how it works:

Stage 1

The initial telephone call confirms company particulars, the number of employees or whatever else is relevant. It also obtains the name – and often the ear – of the decision-maker, so as to introduce the product or service and get agreement to be sent the relevant literature.

Stage 2

A personalized letter and accompanying literature is then sent out by first class post to those whose reactions were positive, advising them to expect a second telephone call either in order to sell to them directly or to make an appointment for a sales person to call in person.

Stage 3

The 'clincher call' comes from four to six days after the mailing.

These three-stage promotions have been used very widely for a variety of organizations, including:

Computer software and hardware;
Car leasing
Business travel
Courier services
Equipment of every kind
Machine tools
Advertising space selling
Advertising and PR services
Accounting management
Office cleaning
Hiring
Credit collection; and
Insurance.

In each case, the prospect list has been clearly defined by the first call, and the name of the decision-maker pinpointed. Whenever the company proves not to be a realistic prospect, its name and address is removed from the list. In the second, or personalized mailing stage, material is posted only to the 'positives' on the list, and when the third stage comes around, the prospect is conversant with the company's services or products and therefore more likely to agree to buy or to see a representative.

Figure 13 Sample script

First telephone call (preceding mailing)

1 Good evening Mr/Mrs . . . ., My name is Mary of the XYZ Painting Company. We are the people who guarantee our outside painting for 25 years. Has your house been painted within the last year, Mr/Mrs . . . .? (yes/no)

a *If yes*: May I send you some literature for future reference then, Mr/Mrs . . . .? (yes/no)

b *If no*: Do you normally have your house painted regularly, Mr/Mrs. . . .? After all, we all have to protect one of the largest investments we ever make in buying a house, don't we? Is yours a 2/3/4-bedroomed house, Mr/Mrs . . . .? (pause for comment)

2 I would like to send you some literature and then phone you back after you've had a chance to look ar it, Mr/Mrs . . . Which day would suit you best? (M/TU/W/Th/F/S)(am/pm)
And which time?

Second telephone call (following mailing)

1 Good evening, Mr/Mrs . . . . This is Mary of XYZ Painting. I'm phoning you as promised. Did you receive our literature?

Our Mr Jones is in your area for the next two weeks. He would like to call on you and discuss the substantial savings that can be made by using XYZ. You are free on a Monday evening or would you prefer another day or time? (M/Tu/W/Th/F/S)(am/pm)

Objections	*Answers*
Can't afford to have my house painted.	XYZ is really inexpensive and is guaranteed for 25 years.
Have to know cost before I allow salesman to come along.	I wish I could tell you, but this does vary considerably. All I do know is that you will save money.
Only had house painted two years ago	How long will it last though, Mr/Mrs. . .? Now is the time to look at XYZ before prices rise again.
Thinking of moving.	Then you're just the person to use XYZ, Mr/Mrs . . . It will without doubt enhance the value of your house.

Comments

The same three-stage technique can be used successfully in consumer promotions.

For example, let us look at a company which offers a long-term outside house painting scheme. By its very nature, its services are expensive, and experience showed the company that it could only expect *houseowners* to be interested in making use of such a service – and not short-term leaseholders who are unlikely to invest money in maintaining a landlord's property.

One of the most difficult things to ask a stranger is, 'Do you own your own house?' All too often, the reply – if there is any at all – is along the lines of 'Mind your own business.' The Phonesell script in this instance therefore had to be particularly soft-sell and the communicators needed to tread very carefully. There are more ways than one, however, of skinning a cat, and question 1 in the script (Figure 13) was carefully designed to eliminate those who were not house-owners, and therefore had no investment to protect.

The subsequent mailing letter was, again, personalized and began by thanking the prospect for his or her time on the telephone, and ended by referring to the fact that a second telephone call would be made in a few days' time.

The personal approach

Direct mail copy, when it is used to follow a telephone call, should be devoid of gimmicks for two important reasons. One is that the prospect has already had the initial discussion and has expressed an interest; he or she will therefore expect to receive the fullest possible details rather than just an 'appetite whetter'.

The other reason is more mundane – the more you spend on the gimmick, the less profitable your campaign becomes. There is a lot of controversy between a short three-and-a-half paragraph message and a two-page letter. Providing, however, that the advantages to the recipient, rather than to the sender, are clearly indicated in the opening paragraphs, and providing that motivation for action is incorporated at the end or in a postscript, I have never found length to be an important factor in response levels.

If the mailing list is on tape, then laser techniques can be used to provide inexpensive personalized letters and contents. At time of writing, this can be done for as little as 14p each. However, the laser industry is in its infancy and it may well be that the price will have altered considerably when this book appears in print.

Alternative personalization is readily and competitively available by use of word processors and auto-typewriters. Where large quantities are needed but the budget is low, a printed letter can be matched with a typed address, using a carbon ribbon typewriter.

The letter should of course be personalized as much as possible, using the various factors which were learned in the first stage telephone call. These personal factors are underlined in the sample letter shown in Figure 14.

An important point to remember — yet often forgotten — is

Figure 14 Appointment letter

The XYZ 25-Year Guaranteed Painting Company
Date _____

Mr J. Brown
211 Courtenay Cresent
Glasgow GL1 4TB

Dear Mr Brown,
Thank you for talking to me on the telephone on <u>Wednesday</u> evening. I did enjoy our chat and, as promised, enclose details of the XYZ 25-year painting plan which is guaranteed to save you a great deal of money on a <u>3-bedroomed</u> house like yours.

As you usually have your house painted every <u>5 years</u>, the XYZ which is probably only slightly more expensive than the old-fashioned method and it will save you four lots of coats. Bearing in mind the high rate of inflation, you will be £s in pocket, and I have no doubt you must agree that the finish of an XYZ painted house is really superior and stands out from its neighbours.

As you asked, I will call you personally on <u>Tuesday</u> evening between <u>7.30 and 8.00 p.m.</u> If this is not convenient, please don't hesitate to call my office which will gladly arrange another time.
I do look forward to speaking with you again and hearing your comments on the literature I've enclosed with this letter.
Yours sincerely
Mary Green

P.S. If we can fix up an appointment before the end of February, we can offer you a 10% discount if you decide to place an order.

---

to eliminate those who spontaneously respond verbally or in writing after receiving the second stage mailer. Calling them as if they had not done so is irritating to the prospect and, of courses, needlessly expensive.

Test the different methods

As in all direct marketing, it is as well to take a small bite of the apple before you swallow a whole fruit which might possibly have a worm hidden inside it. A test of 1000 names and addresses for the XYZ Company could look like this:

	Total	Cost	No. of orders	Cost per order
Mailing 'cold'	250	£100	2	£ 50
Telephoning 'cold'	250	£250	2.5	£100
Telephone and mail follow-up	250	£350	9	£ 39
Three-stage	250	£600	20	£ 30

While a company would deduce that a 'cold' mailing could be more cost-effective than 'cold' telephoning, it is evident that a two-stage combination increases results, while a three-stage promotion, involving perhaps mailing only be 100 of the original 250 telephoned, would prove the most cost-effective method of all.

If, however, it was a video company selling a 'name' video tape to retail stockists, then the same test package could produce entirely different results.

	Total	Cost	No. of tapes sold	Cost per order
Mailing 'cold'	250	£100	40	£2.50
Telephoning 'cold'	250	£250	100	£2.50
Mail and telephone	250	£350	135	£2.60

In this instance, there would be little point in launching a three-stage approach. The video tape distributor would be well advised either to 'cold call' directly by telephone, or to undertake a two-stage promotion – first, by mailing full information, order forms and reply paid envelope, and then following through with a telephone call to the non-respondents.

Telephone and direct mail prove an ideal combination everywhere – and one which is always flexible, speedy, and cost-effective.

12

Market research and the telephone*

Telephone interviewing has its roots in the United States of America, where Dr Gallup started the technique in the late 1920s. It did not become popular, though, until the late 1950s and a number of factors later contributed to its appeal: telephone ownership increased to seven out of ten households and it became clear that personal interviews were both expensive and difficult; speed became more important; Central Telephone Interviewing was invented, and modern computer technology, with its associated advantages, became available.

Although precise figures vary, it is estimated that 80 per cent of households now have access to a telephone in their home, compared with only 40 per cent ten years ago. At that time, the telephone as a research tool was directed mainly at executives and professional people, and used by interviewers in their homes. Although the telephone is still widely used for industrial interviewing, it is becoming increasingly important in conducting consumer interviews.

From a base of virtually zero in 1979 the telephone now accounts for around 9–10 per cent of the total UK research market. It would take a highly cautious accountant to forecast anything other than a continuing rise over the next few years.

Market researchers are somewhat reliant upon norms and therefore any new technique receives a rather sceptical opinion at first. In the early days, the telephone began its route to accep-

* The author and publisher are grateful to Eamonn Santry and Peter Arnold for permission to reproduce material by them in Chapter 12. Eamonn Santry is Managing Director of Telephone Research Limited and a Director of Business Decisions Limited, a member of Aidcom International PLC. The company specializes in telephone techniques for market research purposes. Peter Arnold is a Director of Telephone Research Limited and Business Decisions Limited. His experience of telephone methodologies spans many years and he has written many papers on the subject. Both are pioneers in this recently introduced research method and are at the forefront of new developments.

tability by being used in areas where it was perhaps the only way of economically researching a market or in markets of heavy affluence. Much of this has been owing to the growth of direct marketing. Such a market created vast databases of customers or enquirers of a particular product or service. Telephone research, like direct marketing, is not limited by geography and therefore a database created would probably not be clustered in particular areas. To establish basic reasons for buying or reject- ing would necessitate a veritable army of personal interviewers to cover such an otherwise simple issue. Using the telephone for data collection to customer lists posed not the simple old dichotomy of which method to use, but the question of whether research was to be carried out at all. Telephone is no panacea to all alternative methods and, as with all research methodologies, it has its advantages and disadvantages.

While telephone penetration is now high, a number of points should be considered before opting for, or rejecting, this method of data collection: the data collected by telephone differs from that collected in personal interviews and it is believed that a more honest response to sensitive questions is likely on the telephone. Such interviews are rather remote and therefore less threatening than face-to-face interviews. Here the interviewer may impose a bias, however unintentional. Taking a very simple example: where attitudes of housewives to home cleanliness are sought, what is important is that a respondent *perceives* him/herself as keeping a tidy home. The presence of an interviewer in an opposite environment may lead the housewife to downgrade this perception. Interviewers themselves are not primarily used to check the validity of a respondent's claims, but to record his/her answers to a set of predetermined questions. Thus, there may be a risk that the mere physical presence of a person may impose a certain bias on sensitive issues. Given this logic, great care must be taken in choosing any research technique, not solely telephone methods. However, telephone ownership in itself is biased, and should be questioned on sampling grounds. The 80 per cent telephone penetration figure demonstrates an affluence bias versus the population as a whole. In reality the bias is variable based upon the desired market to be studied. The 80 per cent of telephone homes account for a greater percentage of total market expenditure – around 90 per cent. The bias therefore may be minimal for most FMCG products but the opposite is true when researching rent rebates, single households or the elderly, since the latter are the largest sector of the population without a telephone.

While some bias may be obviated by weighting, care should be taken in this respect, since upweighting a demographic group to the total population figures may only be a cosmetic gesture. The weighting in itself cannot cover non-respondents – i.e. non-telephone owners.

The main attractions of telephone interviewing are speed, cost effectiveness and control. In Telephone Centres, one has total control over the process: personal briefings are carried out on every study; questions proving confusing may be easily changed; supervision and quality checks are carried out during rather than after fieldwork, turnaround times can be reduced to a minimum, and with the introduction of computerization, telephone surveys can be conducted even faster.

Cost effectiveness is a more complex issue. The economies of scale apply to most surveys carried out centrally since all stages of a project are conducted from one location. Telephone research is not necessarily less expensive in all cases – minority samples are one example of this.

Questionnaires need to be worded differently when used on the telephone. One has to develop a rapport with the respondent, and this must be achieved in the first few moments. The interviewer should sound relaxed and friendly and should adopt an informal attitude. Answers to obvious questions should be given before the respondent has time to ask them – why he/she is ringing, who he/she is working for etc. The interviewer's approach is as important as the wording of the questionnaire.

Precoded questions are straightforward, if the interviewer probes properly, but for full answers, he or she must work harder. The use of scales poses few problems and there are basically two modes for this. The first is 'marks out of ten' and the other 'unfolding'.

Four-point scales are easily administered when offered in two parts. First, one asks whether the respondent likes or dislikes that which is to be rated, and then asks, 'by a little or a lot?' The use of five or seven point scales is a little more difficult but one way is to ask the respondent to find a pen and paper and compile lists. The following example can work for batteries of scales and prompted awareness questions:

Question: 'I would like to ask your views on a number of different products. Have you a pen and a piece of paper? I am going to give you the names of a number of products and I would like you to write them down please'.

The interviewer reads out the names on the list and then asks the respondent to read it back. The interviewer should continue when he/she is sure the list is correct and complete.

Question: 'Which of the products shown on your list...?'
'... are best for ...?'
'... have you seen advertised lately?'

Using *Ehrenberg couplets*, this method may be used to administer three-point scales simultaneously for several brands/companies. There is little that cannot be asked on the telephone, provided the questions are asked correctly.

Sampling

There are six main methods of sampling for telephone surveys.

Sampling from previous surveys

Follow-up interviews often add a further dimension to findings. With carefully prepared questionning techniques to avoid conditioning of responses over a period of time, the same sample may be recontacted at fixed intervals to evaluate shifts in attitudes, awareness or purchasing habits. This is not an innovative sampling method, but it illustrates an important use of telephone interviewing.

Sampling from lists

After ensuring that the source list is representative of the area/universe to be sampled, sampling can be carried out using any systematic method.

Random digit dialling*

Random numbers may either be generated manually, within exchange codes using random number tables or, when using Computer Assisted Telephone Interviewing (CATI), by computer random number generators. Although little organized sampling is required, this method is less efficient and therefore less cost-effective, as many of the numbers generated would be non-existent or businesses.

Directory assisted methods

Telephone owners whose numbers are ex-directory will naturally be excluded from a random sample drawn from directories. Telephone numbers in the UK are allocated in blocks and if a number from a directory is chosen, one assumes that it exists. If a new number is generated, by adding one to the original number it is probable that it also exists, i.e. 01-636 2341 becomes 01-636 2342. This does mean, of course, that one samples a proportion of non-existent numbers and a great many business numbers. However, this method does allow unlisted numbers to be sampled and, as a result, gives a good sample of all telephone owners.

This is also a suitable approach for producing perfectly-matched samples, for tracking exercises. After adding one to initial start samples from directories (to produce a Directory Assisted plus One sample for interviewing), a series of matched samples for tracking can be created by adding a further two digits to the Directory Assisted plus One listing. One adds two in preference to one to create each subsequent sample because there are households that have two consecutive telephone numbers, but very few have three.

Random fixed interval sampling

Assuming that one has a set of up-to-date telephone directories, and that one knows how many entries are in each directory, a fixed interval random sample may be drawn. This can be stratified or unstratified, clustered or unclustered. Telephone exchange areas can be used to define standard regions, regional

---

* Random dialling is against the Code of Ethics published in the BDMA Guidelines.

sales areas etc., but by using unclustered samples, sample sizes can be reduced to a minimum.

Solus use of the telephone or combined with other methods

The telephone may be used for many jobs, but any mode of interviewing can become more attractive when combined with other modes of data collection. The following are examples.

Pre-testing radio commercials

In telephone interviewing, the range of audio-stimuli is endless; much hardware is available to play audio tapes over the telephone. It therefore offers an effective means to pre-test radio commercials.

Product placements and recall

Although expensive, product placement studies are generally conducted personally. If one is dealing with lightweight products that can be placed by post, recruitment and recall can be carried out by telephone – a cost-effective method when multiple recalls are needed.

Advertising tracking studies

Essential to effective tracking studies is the ability to produce multiple, perfectly matched samples inexpensively – one advantage of random sampling. The telephone affords great speed and control too, as fieldwork periods can be timed to the hour. It is possible, given the size of telephone centres, to conduct between 500 and 1000 interviews in one evening.

Tactical market evaluation

There is now a growing demand by marketers for answers to tactical issues on a zero lead-time basis. Telephone interviewing has allowed many valuable tactical research projects to be commissioned that at one time would not have been considered.

International projects

This can be useful on a small scale for piloting, group recruitment and investigatory exercises/feasibility studies and, if the interviewers are fluent in the relevant languages, interviews may be conducted with any country.

Although there are restrictions to the use of the telephone for data collection, there are fewer than might be expected. There is a great deal to be learned about the subject though. There are times when, because of sample biases, the method is inappropriate. The length of the interview may be a problem; although it is possible to carry out extensive interviews over the telephone, the subject matter must be interesting.

As telephone penetration increases and more knowledge is amassed, so the use of the telephone as a research tool will expand.

13

Seventeen ways to make the most of your phone

I'm going to try the impossible in this chapter. I'm going to endeavour to list the endless benefits which a professionally-run and well-controlled telephone campaign can provide to just about every kind of organization under the sun – whether it's big business, a political party, a small-town one-man enterprise, a charity, or 'you name it'.

Because the list is 'endless', because any book has space limitations, and because I trust the reader's intelligence to find new and creative ways in which he or she can apply the techniques described in these pages to his or her organization, I'm ending my list arbitrarily after putting down 17 uses for Alexander Graham Bell's magic management tool.

Like your car, the telephone will take you anywhere you want to go. You've just got to learn to drive and point it in the right direction.

Advanced technological developments – such as the new overlay network for the City of London with national and international connections – are making the telephone even more important and useful to every business – indeed, essential to any business wishing to keep ahead in today's tough, competitive climate. These new developments are wonderfully exciting; a great future is in store for us all in the field of telecommunications. Every year – almost every month – brings changes and new developments, even in 'tradition-bound Britain'. The stops are out and the field is wide open, both to the inventive engineer and to British Telecom's competitors.

So, what does the year 2001 hold for us in this respect? And how far have we travelled?

The history of the telephone is rather short, making its rapid development all the more amazing, though these developments have accelerated incredibly within just the past decade or so, thanks to the 'new technology'.

In the very beginning, the user was offered only a very simple system. All calls were directed through the local operator (who became a very popular lady due to her inner knowledge, acquired when she 'forgot' to disconnect from the calls).

Within four years of Alexander Graham Bell's invention, the first patent for automatic switching was granted and the first public telephone exchange began operating, installed in Coleman Street, London, with a total of just eight subscribers!

The genius of Thomas Edison showed itself at this time, and he invented the switchboard.

Although automatic 'switching' was known and indeed actually was in use in Coatbridge, Scotland, in 1886, the British Post Office was in no great hurry to replace the manual arm operator system – despite the fact that more than 20 automatic switching exchanges had been installed in the USA before the year 1900. It was two years before the start of the First World War, in 1912, that the first automatic public telephone exchange in Britain was opened in Epsom, Surrey, with a capacity for serving 500 subscribers.

Here matters rested for a decade. It was in 1922 that the British finally took a lead in telephone development and opened the first public exchange in the world which used automatic relays, at Fleetwood, in Lancashire.

At the end of the 1960s, the Post Office telephone monopoly was broken and private companies were allowed to market Private Automatic Branch Exchanges (PABX) above 100 lines, coinciding with great advances in the usage of the computer. Even more wonderful things began to take shape.

Let's look at just one, which affects the telephone answering machine.

One of the basic advantages of using the telephone is the fact that you have the complete attention of the person at the other end of the line, providing of course that you have been able to connect with the person.

But how many times during this past week have you unsuccessfully tried to get through and speak to someone, failing because the lines were busy or the person was engaged elsewhere or just unavailable? How much did all this cost in terms of your time and possible lost business? Obviously, telephone answering machines partly solve the problem of unavailability, but only in a very limited way.

Soon they'll be outdated. By the year 2001, their only use will be for the consumer market.

A new technique, called 'Voicebank', already operative for some years in San Francisco, and currently installed in London, is a major technological step forward in this field. Voicebank is a computerized programme capable of processing text, data and voice information on a 'store and forward' basis.

With the inception of electronic mail, the Voicebank technique may be used as a 'voice note'. Recipients of the mail will also receive advice that a voice note has been attached. The recipient will then depress a single key and will hear the originator's voice making comments. The full impact of the message will then be made, with no room for error or misunderstanding of the originator's intent.

After 70 years, the Post Office's telephone monopoly has been broken wide open. This has opened up vast areas for exciting growth, and all of us who are in business because we believe in the competitive free enterprise system know what is the natural sequel to competition: we'll be able to expect many more exciting developments by the end of this decade.

This poses a tremendous challenge to management.

In order to meet this new era of telecommunications, management must be made aware that the traditional, face to face meeting in an initial stage of communication – and therefore of selling – is no longer necessary. In fact, it may even be termed obsolete.

The telephone in its present form is a time-saving, highly cost-effective tool. Used under specialist control – by professionals – the telephone *must* increase *any* company's profitability.

Here are 17 uses, each one practical, profitable, and results-orientated:

1   As a substitute

When a geographical area becomes vacant through illness, vacation, or termination of employment, a regular telephone call to customers will keep the business 'live' and ensure that competitors won't creep in through the back door because of a lack of contact by your company.

2   Testing a mailing list

My experience of handling more than 1500 computer files of major mailing lists shows that the telephone can be a very good testing ground for any such mailing list.

We have found that a good formula is 50 calls per 1000 names and addresses. The use of the telephone is far cheaper than testing a list by means of a mailing, because of the lower quantity needed, and of course the answers come back much more quickly.

If, for example, you intended to rent a list purported to be of 250,000 parents with children under the age of 5, or of detached house-owners, or companies owning main-frame computers, then the veracity and potential worth of that list can easily and speedily be checked by telephone.

3   Fundraising

One of the first UK charities to understand the potential value of the telephone in terms of increased income was Dr Barnardo's Homes. Their training officer, John Kelson, became so involved in the successful use of the telephone as a fund-raising medium that he eventually became the first Chairman of the Telephone Council of the British Direct Marketing Association. It has been proved that the telephone is a very successful method of raising funds for any charity, institution, or other fundraising scheme, whether it involves selling tickets to a policeman's ball or direct contributions to building funds etc. One fairly large organization, for example, annually sells thousands of magazine subscriptions by telephone, after advising prospects that a percentage of the monies received is being donated to specific charities.

It is now not uncommon for businesses to receive at least one call a month asking them to sponsor a balloon race or a 20 mile walk on behalf of various good causes.

4   Test marketing

Where a good basic list is available, test marketing by

telephone can be low-cost, flexible in terms of demographics, unbiased by person-to-person reactions, and very speedy.

An overseas manufacturer wished to launch his innovative water irrigation system in Denmark. The company had very little knowledge of the Scandinavian agricultural industry, but decided that before appointing agents it would be beneficial to have a detailed idea of the scope and need for the product.

A Danish telephone bureau was employed to make contact with 500 farmers owning large acreages. They were questioned on their existing methods of irrigation and their attitudes towards possible purchase of the new product. At the same time they were also asked to give details of the machinery agents whom they favoured when purchasing any new equipment.

Following the completion of this exercise, sufficient positive information was received to encourage the overseas manufacturer to make the necessary investment to launch the product. The next stage was the establishment of likely agencies, and using the information gained from the first exercise, a second telephone test marketing exercise was organized in which the possible prospective agents were asked various questions necessary in order to narrow the field sufficiently before the final choice was made. Upon completion of this second test, the results were analysed and a third telephone marketing promotion was arranged in order to make firm qualified appointments with a short-list of likely candidates.

The managing director of the manufacturer then visited Denmark for two weeks and was able in this time to finalize his arrangements, having selected the agency with whom he wished to work.

Total cost of this test marketing before the launch of a new product was just £5500. Had they not chosen to use the telephone, the operation could have been expected to involve an expenditure of around £15,000 with no guarantee that the end result could not have been total failure.

Testing anything by telephone must make sense – demographic, pricing structure, geographical bias, product, timing, mailing list, or need.

Research comes into many test projects. For example, one manufacturer wished to test the market for a new, low-priced chocolate bar within a particular TV area. We telephoned 500 confectionery retailers to ask if they would take part in a six-week survey during which time they would be supplied with some outers of the chocolate for display on their counters.

We explained what this entailed. Each week, these retailers would be telephoned and asked eight or nine different market research questions; at the end of the six-week period each retailer who took part would receive £5 for his trouble (and of course be charged for the number of chocolate bars actually sold). 415 retailers agreed to take part in the survey. Seven 'dropped out' along the way and the remainder continued until the end of the scheme.

This telephone test marketing effort cost the manufacturer a total of £7000. The same results, obtained in more conventional, old-fashioned ways, would probably have cost around £15,000 to £20,000.

5 Investigation

The speed of the telephone is phenomenal. There are some forms of investigation which can produce results in just one day when undertaken by telephone – that can make all the difference to a company's success or failure.

The case history which leaps to my mind is that of a multinational electrical manufacturer with huge profits in all but one division of its group. This loss-making division was obviously a thorn in the side of management, and the directors issued instructions that the whole division would be closed down unless the situation was put right immediately.

The company's 'whizz-kid' was asked to look into the situation and it was he who approached my organization, asking us to contact 1500 electrical wholesalers with the objective of discovering the reason why there was a drop in demand for what was, and is, an excellent product.

On the side, as it were, we were also told to note the requirements of any customer who wished to place an order. Finally, just before the campaign commenced, we were also told that the manufacturer had been about to launch a new (and as yet unnamed) electrical gadget onto the marketplace. Without any literature available, we were given a description of the product and its price and were asked to mention the gadget to the wholesalers.

The whole project took place in one day. The result was startling.

1375 contacts immediately answered the company's- basic question − .why had the division lost its share of the marketplace? The answer was simple. The company had an inadequate salesforce, with an infrequent calling pattern. This fact had made it possible for the company's more aggressive competitors to take a larger slice of what was a fairly limited cake.

With the facts from these 1375 reports available, our client therefore was able quickly to put matters right and bring the division back into profit fairly readily.

Interestingly, during the same exercise, we took in orders for the existing products totalling more than £10,000. And, as a bonus to a very successful and worthwhile exercise, we sold, sight unseen, a further £4000 of the new product!

Yet the whole telephone campaign cost the manufacturer at that time (1979) only £1500.

6   Testing campaign penetration

The telephone is a very capable ally in finding out the extent to which an advertising campaign has penetrated.

You may be heavily committed to large TV and print media budgets, and the results of these should soon be reflected in your sales, but until you know the extent of the penetration of your campaign, can you really be sure that the approaches adopted are giving you the best value for your money?

As a manufacturer of a washing-up liquid, does your product also appeal to farmers' wives and grandmothers? Are they even aware of your product? Has your advertising made its impact?

If you are a commercial stationers, advertising in all the trade journals, would it not be worthwhile finding out if your prospects are aware of your inventory?

Testing the market isn't only useful for a company. It makes sense for any organization dealing with the public. One major

British charity, in existence for more than a century, with an excellent management structure, comes to mind as an example. This highly respected organization undertakes much-needed family social work, both in visiting the homes of needy families (needy in the sense of emotional as well as financial support) and in the maintenance of homes for the aged. However, contributions had not been widely forthcoming from the community, and there appeared to be a certain lethargy towards this charity, despite the continuous educational advertisements which it placed in the relevant press.

We made 500 telephone calls for this charity, asking questions along the lines of, 'Do you know what work this charity does?' and 'Is there a specific reason why you would not support it with contributions?'

Again, the answer became clear during the course of *just one evening* – the length of time it took us to conduct this campaign. The public was simply unaware of the extent of the charity's social work activities! Obviously, the charity's advertising had *not* succeeded in its objective – which was to educate.

The charity took the lesson to heart and began doing something about it, with success reflected in substantially higher donations.

7   Obtain qualified appointments

As I pointed out in Chapter 1, where I discussed the cost of keeping a salesman on the road, prospecting for qualified appointments by telephone makes good economic sense.

Finding examples is difficult, but only because the choice is so wide. I cannot think of any commercial or consumer direct-sell product or service whose sales cannot be cost-effectively increased by using the telephone to separate the good prospect from the time-waster with the representative being used solely to do the job for which he is employed – selling.

Take an everyday office need such as a photocopying machine. A hard-working salesman in a densely commercially-populated area could expect to sit in 12 waiting rooms every day, cooling his heels, and may be lucky enough to elicit interest from three prospects, who actually allow him to demonstrate his equipment. At the end of the week, from the 15 demonstrations, perhaps he's lucky enough to get five sales.

If, however, his company had used the telephone on his behalf, then instead of 15 actual demonstrations resulting in five sales per week, he would have had 60 firm appointments with interested prospects during the same period. Eliminating time-wasting 'cold' calling, he could have made 20 sales.

The prospects would have been those people who had actually expressed an interest in having a new photocopier; each of them would have been prepared, well before the salesman's arrival, seriously to discuss the possibility of purchasing.

8 Repetitive selling

If you are selling the same product every week to the same customer list, be it cassette tapes, drink, confectionery, tobacco, ice cream or any merchandise, why waste the time of your sales force by converting them into order takers?

An example is provided by a multinational company which sells its products into do-it-yourself, hardware and paint shops, as well as into department stores. They analysed their business and came to the conclusion that 90 per cent of it was repetitive selling. Their product was in fact the brand leader, a household name, and they had penetrated 80 per cent of all possible outlets.

After a considerable amount of testing, a training scheme was inaugurated for Regional Telephone Sales Supervisors, which was followed by the employment of about 100 home telephone owners. These people in turn were trained very thoroughly in the company's products and taught phoneselling. Each person now works from their own home, with a small microcomputer installation and very stringently-maintained reporting procedures. Within the first 6 months, sales rose by 35 per cent and subsequently continued upward. Because of the low cost of obtaining the sales by telephone, profit margins doubled.

9 Motivate lapsed customers

Your very best prospect file is the one which has the names of your lapsed customers. What's happened to them? Has their business changed hands, and, if so, have the new owners been asked for their custom? Were they offended with something your company did, or had left undone – and has anything been done about smoothing things down? Have they been told about new lines, schemes, opportunities? Above all, has anyone actually asked why they no longer give you their custom? And does the customer know that their business is valued by your organization?

Good questions, I think you'll agree. Sadly, they're questions a lot of companies don't bother asking. And they're all questions which are easy to ask over the telephone.

That's something which a department store in France learned to its profit. It re-activated 42 per cent of all its lapsed account customers by telephoning to say the things we've just mentioned. Their campaign was linked to a special offer along the lines of, 'A magnificent percolator will be sent free of charge if you place an order now, just to show how much we value your custom'.

Where resistance was met with, due to a real or imagined grievance from the past, this was dealt with speedily and professionally and client goodwill was ensured.

10   Preceding and/or following a direct mail campaign

For companies involved in direct-mail campaigns, the telephone is an ideal 'insurance policy'. It should be used to precede the campaign and to qualify the company's prospect file, while at the same time updating and clarifying its mailing list. This eliminates the non-starters. The 'golden rule' here is don't send your expensive mailers to those who will never be your customers.

Use the telephone call to find out:

- If there is awareness of what you have to offer;
- Whether there's a possible need for your product/service;
- What company demographics would be applicable to your sales pitch;
- The name(s) of the decision-maker(s).

11 New launch

A vigorous promotion agency was asked to help in the launch of a new milk-based drink. This was aimed at the teen to twenties age group.

Some very striking advertising had been shown on Granada TV and the promotion agency was backing this with both direct mail and field sales selling face-to-face.

Because the initial consignment of the drinks were date-stamped, time was of the very essence in this launch – and the agency decided to use telephone marketing to follow through on the mailing campaign. Some 6000 CTNs were contacted in the Granada TV area to coincide with the TV launch. The shops were asked to purchase some cases of the drinks in order to meet the demand which was being generated. As an added, but small incentive, a £1 discount was offered when two or more cases were purchased. Several tons of the product were sold in this way.

New products, schemes, colours, sizes or ideas can quickly and effectively be launched by telephone to a list of existing or peripheral customers.

'We want you to be one of the first to know that...' is a very positive approach which, by insinuation, combines flattery and education to produce a high level of orders – and all without incurring the costs inherent to face-to-face selling. This also applies, of course, to the promotion of special merchandise to generate store traffic.

These lessons don't only apply to big business. Portrait photographers specializing in family pictures provide another example. Many of them annually visit towns and villages, taking their cameras directly into the homes of their clients. Six weeks before their proposed visit, they habitually send a mailing to previous and prospective clients, enclosing a reply-paid card asking for convenient dates and times to be notified if the clients wish to have some photographs taken.

This horse-and-buggy approach worked successfully for several years until they decided to try the effect of a full scale phone-in, following a mailing to their previous prospective list file. The results were astonishing: their bookings increased substantially and the small, but irritating percentage of non-fulfilled appointments almost disappeared.

12   Sale of surplus stock

A major distributor of toys who had the UK franchise for a well-known electronic game, undertook extensive TV and press advertising in the weeks prior to Christmas, in order to generate sales for the large volume of games due to be delivered at the beginning of November. To their horror an expected large consignment of the merchandise did not arrive as planned, but was belatedly delivered only on 15 December – too late for distribution in the normal way.

This meant that most of the stock would not be sold for some months, resulting in serious cash-flow problems for the company. The only solution was to contact 4200 retailers very quickly, endeavouring to put forward a proposal attractive enough to encourage them to buy so near to Christmas.

Seventy telephone communicators were employed to contact the toy shops during the course of one day – 16 December. Each prospect was offered the inducement of a 'baker's dozen' – 13 games for every 12 ordered – as well as extended credit terms, with payments not being required until the end of January. Delivery was promised within two days, and the company's sales force was used to undertake this. By the end of 16 December, each piece of merchandise had been sold and was actually in the retail outlet by the 18th.

13   Converting enquiries to sales

How many advertisements actually attract your interest to such an extent that you fill in coupons and send for further information or samples, or both? And what happens after you have done so?

In most of the cases, you'll either place an order or not – it's as simple as that. Yet on those occasions when your enquiry is followed through by a telephone call in order to encourage and motivate you to proceed with a purchase, there is certainly a strong likelihood that you will do so.

The cost-effectiveness of this kind of promotion is dependent upon the product being offered and the seriousness of the original enquiry, and also the length of time which has elapsed until the follow-up contact is made.

All telephone marketing costs must be carefully monitored on an hourly basis, and particularly careful records should be maintained in order to develop the most effective pattern.

An example is provided by a passenger shipping line which produced a list of 1800 people who in January 1982 had asked for details of the line's spring cruise. Their names were later checked against the ultimate passenger list, and those who were not taking part in the cruise were to be contacted in January 1983 and asked if they were still interested in a spring cruise.

180 telephone contacts, a random 10 per cent of the total, revealed that the cost of following up after one year was *not* justified, and that the original enquiry had been made purely on impulse.

However, a tour operator specializing in winter sports who undertook exactly the same type of promotion found that the cost proved very justified – with an incredible 8.5 per cent of all those being contacted converting to firm bookings.

14   Incoming calls

Incoming direct orders and bookings must be taken just as professionally and controlled in the same way as any outgoing telephone campaign.

This applies, whether the incoming telephone call resulted from TV, radio, direct mail or point-of-sale advertising. Don't empty order-takers, but ensure that the telephones are answered by trained communicators able to perform their task – which is to sell, sell and sell.

Every opportunity is provided by this unique voice-to-voice situation to enable you to take advantage of the complete attention of the enquiree at the other end of the receiver. If the request is for a brochure, the communicator should, if this is relevant, give the address of the nearest stockist. Where an order is being placed, perhaps for a children's paddling pool, then the communicator ought also to try and sell swings, deckchairs, or whatever other items of this kind are stocked. If it is a retailer calling to order three cases of chocolate bars, then encourage the caller to buy 9 or 12 cases, by detailing the savings. Should the enquirer be interested in a service, a holiday, insurance policy, private health scheme, then make sure the benefits are sold enthusiastically.

15 Inviting the prospect to a seminar

There are many larger items which cannot be sold without the benefit of a demonstration actually on site – but telephone selling is an excellent method of extending invitations to seminars, exhibitions and informative selling sessions.

One multinational computer manufacturer imaginatively organized a train to travel throughout Western Europe, stopping for two to three days in each major city, where their mainframe computer was demonstrated. Telephone marketers were used in each country two weeks prior to the scheduled visit in order to contact likely prospects, encourage interest wherever possible, and extend invitations to visit the exhibition at specific times.

Thousands of prospects took advantage of the proposal, and a very satisfactory level of sales were achieved, basically because the attendees in this instance all fell into one category of likely purchasers, certain parameters being established at the time of the original telephone call.

If, however, the invitations had been issued on an ad hoc basis throughout the usual media, there is no doubt that whilst the quantity of attendees might have been larger, the quality, in terms of definite prospects, would have been lower and the demonstrators' attention would have had to be spread thinly on the ground – with resultant fewer sales.

16 Political purposes

In the United States, telephone marketing has for many years figured very prominently in electioneering budgets and I have very little doubt that it will do so also in the United Kingdom when next the country goes to the polling booths.

It is not unusual in America to receive a telephone call with a friendly voice saying out of the blue, 'Mr Brown? Hello there, the President would just like to say a few words to you about the election....' This is then followed by a familiar (taped) voice giving the particular message.

Thousands of these combination live-and-taped calls are made daily and the response is said to be very satisfactory overall. The taped voice can be and often is that of a famous show business personality expounding the particular cause.

Taped messages of this kind are not only useful for political campaigns, but can be used to provide a testimonial for charities, products, services, holidays, real estate – in fact providing a method of motivating public opinion which can be used to promote virtually anything.

17 Direct selling

Anything from a £15 subscription to a £30,000 crane can be sold by telephone. I know – we've done it.

Providing the ground rules are followed carefully, direct sales can be concluded cost-effectively. It is particularly important to make the offer in a clear, honest and natural way – and to recapitulate by confirming in the exact instructions, so that the customer is absolutely sure of the terms and conditions relating to the sale.

In circumstances where the communicator is working on a commission basis, it is often advisable to use a verifier, whose job it is to qualify the sale. It would be unwise to convey to the client that a second call is being made for this specific purpose and verifiers should use gambits such as:

- 'We'd just like to confirm the delivery address.'
- 'Did we mention that you have a choice of colours?'
- 'Can I verify your name for invoice purposes?'

In view of the fact that it is undoubtedly easy for a prospect to place an order on the telephone which he or she may later repent, and possibly deny, it can save time and money if a verification call is made before the dispatch of a high-value order.

There is no end to the ways in which the telephone can become your greatest asset in business – providing that it is handled professionally and given the time, the respect and the attention it deserves.

But remember: you do need more than a desk, a phone, and a body.

Much more.

Index

advertising campaign penetration,
  testing, 127–8
appointments, obtaining for
  salesmen, 16–17, 128–9
automatic switching, 122

BDMA Telephone Council,
  29–30, 65, 66, 124
benefits, emphasizing, 49, 50, 72,
  78, 79–80
bonus payments, 55
Borris, Sir Gordon, 66
British Direct Marketing
  Association Telephone
  Council, 29–30, 65, 66, 124
brochure requests, 89
Broidy, Gerry, 19
business call contact rates, 24

call cards, 25
call logging, 99
call reporting see records
clerical staff, 25, 38
closing a sale, 81
commission, 27, 53–4
communicators
  clerical back-up required by,
    25, 38
  compared with face to face
    salesperson, 17–18
  data prep training, 92
  incentives for, 23, 27, 45, 53–7
  incoming calls answered by, 87,
    88, 93, 133–4
  managers recruited from, 39

objections answered by see
  objections, dealing with
part-time, 40, 41
payment, 27, 53–4
records for, 23, 44–6
recruitment, 41–4
removal of ineffective workers,
  24–5, 40–1
results displayed, 37
scripts for see
  scripts/scriptwriting
working environment and
  conditions, 17, 36–8, 57
Computel machines, 94, 96
Computer Assisted Telephone
  Interviewing, 118
computerization, 25–7, 92–101
  call logging, 99
  computer software, 100
  computer telephones, 93–9
  data prep training, 92
  graphs produced, 26, 27
  integration of voice and data,
    93
  link to central computer, 92
  personally worded letters, 26,
    27
computer software, 100
computer telephones, 93–9
  as instrument of research, 94
  available equipment, 94
  cost, 97–9
  incoming calls and, 97
  possibility of misuse, 96
  script, 95

sequential dialling, 96
techniques, 97
used in USA, 94, 95, 96, 97
consumer response hours, 24, 65
consumer retail location service,
90
contests, 55
cost-effectiveness, 22–7
call cards, 25
computers, 25–7
effective deployment of
communicators, 25
intangible costs, 22, 23
payment, 27
records necessary, 23, 24
removal of incompetent staff,
24–5
response hours, 24
tangible costs, 22
coupons, 86, 105

data prep training, 92
dealer location service, 89–90
direct mail and telephone, 18–20,
103–113, 130
advantages of the combination,
18, 130
mailing as the first stage, 103–5
marketing situations, 102
personalization, 110–112
telephone call as first stage, 19,
105–7
testing different methods,
112–3
three stage (phone-mail-phone),
20, 107–110
directory assisted sampling
methods, 118
DSN, 88
duplication, avoidance of, 65–6

earphones, 25, 92
enquiries, converting into sales,
132–3

face to face calls see salesmen
financial information by phone,
89
Freephone, 87
fundraising, 124
furniture/furnishings for
telephone marketing
department, 37–8

graphs, 26, 27
guidelines for telephone
marketing bureaux, 29–30, 66

harassment, 52
headphones, 25, 92

incentives
for prospective buyers, 90, 103
for staff, 23, 27, 45, 53–7
incoming calls
advantages of giving phone
numbers in advertisements,
86–7
computerization and, 93, 97, 99
DSN, 88
Freephone, 87
importance of good
communicators, 87, 88, 133–4
planning an incoming call
service, 90–1
RCF, 87–8
success stories, 88–90
transcription, 91
in-house telephone marketing
department, 32, 33–47
analysing results, 45–7
cost per annum, 35–6
job functions, 38–41
records, 44–7
recruitment, 41–4
setting up the department, 36–8
telephone marketing bureaux
and, 32, 33–5
test campaigns, 33–5

intangible costs, 22, 23
international projects, 119
interview form, 41, 42–3
investigation, telephone used for, 126–7

Kelson, John, 124

lapsed customers, motivating, 129–30
launching new products, 131–2
leads for salesmen, 16–17, 46–7, 128–9
letters, 26, 27, 110–111
list brokers, 59–63
lists, 58–66, 117, 124
  avoiding duplication, 65–6
  categories, 58–63
  market research sampling from, 117
  random dialling, 66
  testing, 63–5, 124
  timing and, 65

mailing lists, testing, 124 see also lists
mail preference scheme, 64
making the most of the telephone see uses of telephone campaigns
manager, 38–9
market place, changes in the, 13–14
market research by telephone, 17, 114–20
  advantages of, 116
  bias, 115–6
  compared with personal interviews, 115
  cost effectiveness, 116
  increase in, 114
  questionnaires, 116–7
  sampling methods, 117–9

use of telephone on its own or combined with other data collection methods, 119
media advertising, 13, 20, 127
motivation of staff by incentives, 23, 27, 45, 53–7

negative responses see objections, dealing with

objections, dealing with, 48–52, 70–1, 78, 83–5
OFT Report on Telephone Selling (1984), 66
oil prices, effect of increases in, 13
Organization of Petroleum Exporting Countries (OPEC), 13, 14

participation, 57
personalization, 110–112
political uses for telephone, 95–6, 134–5
postal charges, 13–14
Private Automatic Branch Exchanges (PABX), 122
product placements and recall, 119
promotion, staff, 56
publications, industrial and commercial, 58–9
public telephone exchanges, history of, 122

questionnaires, market research, 116–7

radio commercials, pre-testing, 119
random dialling, 66, 96, 118
random fixed interval sampling, 118–9
RCF, 87–8

records, 23, 24, 44–7
  analysing results, 23, 24, 45–7
  communicator's daily call
    report, 44, 45
  importance of, 44–5
  response hours shown by, 24
  weekly management call record
    card, 46
  weekly mangement sales leads
    report, 47
recruitment, 41–4
remote call forwarding service,
  87–8
repetitive selling, 129
resistance *see* objections, dealing
  with
response hours, 24, 65
rules, staff, 37

salaries, communicators', 27,
  53–4
salesmen
  compared with telephone
    communicators, 15–16,
    17–18, 68, 69
  costs, 14, 16
  objections heard by, 70
  obtaining leads for, 16–17,
    46–7, 128–9
  telephone used to fill gaps in
    representation by, 31, 123
  mentioned, 107, 127
sampling methods for telephone
  surveys, 117–9
scripts/scriptwriting
  basic rules, 71–4
  closing a sale, 81
  computer software and, 100
  computer telephones, 95
  emphasizing benefits, 78, 79–80
  objections and, 70–1, 78, 83–5
  overcoming resistance, 83–5
  overcoming the secretarial
    hurdle, 75–6

  sample scripts discussed, 74–83,
    104, 109, 110
  scripts used as guidelines, 67–8
  skills required by scriptwriter,
    68
  testing and adjusting, 20, 21,
    23, 57, 73–4
  three stage approach (phone-
    mail-phone), 74–5, 109, 110
  useful phrases, 80
  word pictures, 68–9, 72
secretaries, getting past, 75–6
seminars, invitations to, 134
setting up in-house telephone
  marketing department, 33–47
staff, 36, 38–41 *see also*
  communicators
substitute, telephone as, 31, 123
supervisor, 38, 39–40, 56
surplus stock, sale of, 132
switchboard, invention of, 122

tactical market evaluation, 119
tangible costs, 22
targets, 23
technological developments,
  121–3
telephone answering machines,
  122–3
telephone marketing bureaux,
  28–32, 33–5
  experience, 28–9
  gap in representation and, 31
  guidelines, 29–30
  in-house department and, 32
  marketing know-how, 29
  payment, 30–1
  personnel, 30
  procedures, 30
  size, 29
  test campaigns conducted by,
    33–5
  when to use, 31, 32
test campaigns, 33–5

testing
  advertising campaign
    penetration, 127–8
  incoming call system, 90–1
  lists, 63–5, 124
  sales techniques, 20–1
  scripts, 20, 21, 57, 73–4
  see also test campaigns; test
    marketing
test marketing, 124–6
three stage (phone-mail-phone)
  approach, 74–5, 107–110
timing, 24, 65
tracking studies, 119
transcription, 91

USA
  automatic switching in, 122
  computerized telephones used
    in, 94, 95, 96, 97
  computer software in, 100
  market research, 114
  origins of phoneselling in, 12
  political use of phone, 94–5,
    134–5
uses of telephone campaigns,
  121–36
  as a substitute, 123
  converting enquiries to sales,
    132–3

direct selling, 135
fundraising, 124
incoming calls, 133–4
investigation, 126–7
inviting prospect to seminar,
  134
motivating lapsed customers,
  129–30
new launch, 131–2
obtaining qualified
  appointments, 128–9
political purposes, 134–5
repetitive selling, 129
sale of surplus stock, 132
testing campaign penetration,
  127–8
testing a mailing list, 124
test marketing, 124–6
with direct mail campaigns, 130

verification, 135
Voicebank, 123

winning combination, 103–113
  see also direct mail and
    telephone
word pictures, 68–9
working conditions and
  environment, 17, 36–8, 57